BETTY COPE, WVIZ,
and the
GREATEST SHOW ON AIR

BETTY COPE, WVIZ,
——— *and the* ———
GREATEST SHOW ON AIR

CHRISTINE L. MARTUCH

THE
History
PRESS

Published by The History Press
Charleston, SC
www.historypress.com

First published 2024

Manufactured in the United States

ISBN 9781467156592

Library of Congress Control Number: 2023950832

To God the Father, Son, and Holy Spirit, Whose wisdom provided me with unfailing guidance throughout this project.
To my husband, Bob, whose love, natural inquisitiveness, boundless enthusiasm, and eager assistance served to encourage me through this endeavor. The Auction was our special time.
To my parents, Trudy and Pete Simko, who taught me the importance of hard work and discipline. Dakujem.

Contents

Acknowledgements

Many individuals graciously shared their time, memories, and photographs to bring the story of Betty Cope's life to fruition. I am most deeply indebted to the entire Henry family, namely, Heidi Henry Cregar, Chris Henry, KC Henry, Rick Henry, Scott Henry, and Robyn Henry. Thank you so much for your hospitality at the family cabin and for allowing us to become a part of your lives. Your retellings of the Cope and Henry family histories have enriched us immensely. Your recollections of experiences with your Aunt Betty certainly brought her to life for this book.

Thank you to Mrs. Edna Strnad, who remembered the "Girl with the TV Antenna Sticking Out of Her Head."

I am certainly grateful to Candy Lee Korn and Bunny Breslin for sharing their memories of Betty Cope as well as wonderful photos depicting the earliest days of Ohio's first television station, WEWS.

A special thank-you must be extended to Ted Lux, whose WVIZ Auction memories are an absolute delight. Your kindness, enthusiasm, and willingness to share your time and precious photos revealed that you are truly just as nice as you sound on the radio.

I am especially appreciative of Mrs. Terry Kovel for spending an afternoon with us reminiscing about her friendship with Betty Cope, her work, and the Auction. Terry Kovel is a priceless treasure.

For sharing your stories about the "Greatest Show on Air," I am most grateful to WVIZ Auction chairperson Dianne Miller; auctioneers Myron

Xenos, Jim Szymanski, and Sherrill Paul Witt; and Art Board volunteer Laurel Kest. Thanks also to Carter Edman, who provided stunning photographs of his mother, Carol Bosley, at the Auction. I am also thankful to Wayne Homren of Numismatic Bibliomania for locating photos of Myron Xenos. The story of Betty Cope could not be told without the story of the Auction!

Many thanks to all of those who worked most closely with Betty Cope at WVIZ, particularly Frank Strnad and Mark Rosenberger. Thanks to you, we have learned a great deal about the workings of the educational station that Betty helped establish nearly sixty years ago.

Retired engineer Larry Tressler painted the most colorful picture of the beginnings of public broadcasting in Cleveland. Thank you, Larry, for your excellent reminiscences about Max Hayes and the Brookpark Road studios.

I am very grateful to Gary Bluhm, Dick Barnick, Gary Manke, Terry Manke, and Gary Valente for explaining many behind-the-scenes technical aspects of broadcasting at WVIZ. I now have a greater appreciation of the intricacies of television production.

Thank you, Rich Cochran, for sharing your recollections of Betty's role as a mentor to you at the Western Reserve Land Conservancy. Also, I am extremely appreciative of Dr. Mark Rzeszotarski, John Leech, and Tom Curtin for their reminiscences of Betty Cope and her work at the Geauga Park District. Thank you also to Dottie Drockton and Sandy Ward for providing photos of Betty at Geauga Park District functions.

I owe a debt of gratitude also to Beth Piwkowski of Cleveland State University Library and Caryn Hilfer of Advance Ohio for locating and providing archival photographs of Betty Cope and other significant historical figures.

Finally, a tip of the hat to Daniel Smith and Brandy Arnold of Familyography in Parma, Ohio, for your prompt service in scanning numerous old Cope family photographs and transferring VHS tapes to a portable drive. Thank you very much for your professional assistance.

CLM

Introduction

Nestled in the woods of Bainbridge Township, Ohio, along the quiet Aurora Branch of the Chagrin River, lies an unassuming wood cabin. In the rear of this cabin, there is a laundry room, one wall of which is completely covered with bronze and marble awards and varnished tribute plaques. The cabin's owner had been named a member of the Journalism Hall of Fame and the Cleveland Inter-Club's Woman of the Year, was awarded several honorary degrees, and received numerous other professional accolades. In the living room at the front of this cabin stands an illuminated antique art deco–style curio cabinet. Prominently on display in this cabinet, next to a Broadcasting Emmy award, is a life-size glass apple, the inscription on which reads, "With Thanks and Love," from inner-city high school students whom she taught the fine art of television production. It was of this glass apple that the cabin owner was most proud. Betty Cope, you see, was first, an educator.

While Betty Cope's name and face are well known by many of Cleveland's baby boomer television viewers, the story of this Cleveland pioneer broadcaster and public television founder is not. It was because of Betty that Cleveland's children in the 1950s watched their first TV programs with Uncle Jake and Texas Jim, and homemakers kept their figures by exercising with Paige Palmer. Perhaps more significantly, due to Betty, thousands of Cleveland-area children learned to spell and count by watching *Sesame Street*. Thanks to Betty, some of those children were likely inspired to study math and science by watching *Cosmos* and *Nova* or literature by watching Masterpiece Theatre.

Dave Garroway, the first host of NBC's *Today Show*, once noted that "the television audience is the largest classroom in the world." If this is true, Betty Cope was not only its teacher but also its school principal. Betty's zeal for education and sharp business savvy combined to make her arguably the most ambitious person in the history of Cleveland television. While some might consider her as a trailblazer for women in television, Betty did not consider herself a feminist. Rather she was an individualist who prided herself in doing her best to present quality educational television programs.

Perhaps subconsciously, the placement of her broadcasting awards in the utility room of her home illustrated her attitude of "just doing her job." But for Betty, it was more than a job; it was a mission to serve the people of Cleveland. At the same time, she managed Cleveland's public television station as a successful business. Her strong organizational acumen and love for education manifested themselves in the form of an annual televised fundraising event that was beloved by the entire community for decades.

Each year, the "organized chaos," as Betty affectionately called the WVIZ Televised Auction, raised more funds for the station than any other source of funding. High-powered antennae and satellite dishes were purchased through Auction funds, enabling WVIZ to increase its broadcasting capacity. For Northeast Ohioans, the Auction provided not only a way of obtaining valuable antiques, quirky collectibles, and useful household items but also a means of sustaining their favorite public TV station. Over the years, thousands of loyal volunteers worked together to put the show on the air. It was also an unpredictable, wildly entertaining, and educational home

Betty Cope's glass apple of appreciation from John F. Kennedy High School in Cleveland. *Author's collection.*

shopping experience for Clevelanders. It was old-style live television with purpose and a modern twist.

Education was the thread that wove together Betty's three loves: television, her family, and the land, particularly Cleveland. Upon leaving WVIZ in 1993, Betty was appointed commissioner of the Geauga Park District and became a trustee of the Chagrin River Land Conservancy. But it was as "First Lady of the Auction" that Clevelanders best remember Betty Cope. The WVIZ Auction showcased her three loves and ultimately helped to create her legacy in public television history. This is the story of Betty Cope, broadcasting pioneer, and the unique way that she kept her station running.

1

Lessons from a Self-Made Man

The seeds of ambition that sprouted WVIZ were actually rooted in Cleveland in 1897, for to tell the story of Betty Cope, one must begin by telling the story of her father. Iri Cope was the very model of a self-made twentieth-century man. His determined, entrepreneurial spirit propelled his efforts to grow a tiny local printing company into a successful mail-order advertising business, ultimately reaching thousands of homes across the country. Undoubtedly, the enterprising Iri inspired his progressive daughter to chart a course in a new electronic medium. As granddaughter Heidi Henry Cregar stated, "Iri and Betty were cut from the same cloth."

The man who had the greatest influence on Betty Cope's life was born Iri Reynolds Cope in Cleveland on July 24, 1897, to William Milhous Cope and Lucy Reynolds Cope. As a youngster, he grew up in the Nottingham neighborhood of Euclid. By 1910, the family had moved to East Cleveland. Iri graduated from Shaw High School in 1915. At the outbreak of war in 1917, Iri and several of his Shaw High friends enlisted in the army. Iri reached the rank of corporal in September 1917 and was promoted to sergeant by June 1918. Iri served in the Defensive Sector of the American Expeditionary Forces from June 1918 to March 1919 at Meuse-Argonne and received an honorable discharge on March 15, 1919.

Among the Shaw High friends with whom Iri enlisted was one Benson Shupe, whose younger sister Marcella charmed Iri. Marcella, who was born in Cleveland in 1903, was also a product of Shaw and later graduated from Swarthmore College. On November 8, 1922, Marcella Shupe and Iri

Iri Cope, Betty's father, at age seven, circa 1900. *Henry family collection.*

Cope were married at the Church of the Covenant in Cleveland. Their first residence was on Eddy Road in East Cleveland.

In July 1923, Iri, together with local businessman Ralph J. Bishop and attorney Melville W. Vickery, founded the Bishop-Cope Printing Company Inc. Located at 2530 Superior Avenue, Bishop-Cope's primary product was direct mail advertising. Catalogue sales from Montgomery Ward and Sears Roebuck were a booming business in postwar America, and Iri jumped on the shop-from-home bandwagon.

Another boom of postwar era was the Florida real estate bubble. After starting the initial printing business, the ever-venturous Iri purchased a 1,200-acre tung tree plantation in Monticello, Florida. Pressing the seed of the tung tree produces tung oil, which is used in wood varnishes.

Besides growing his businesses in the 1920s, Iri's family was growing as well. Daughter Janet was born on August 26, 1924, and Elizabeth was born on December 20, 1925. The family resided on Dorchester Road in Shaker Heights, Ohio. Around 1932, an incident at this house changed their lives forever. One day, their mischievous pet German shepherd chased a stray cat through an open door into their house. The panicked cat scrambled up a curtain and leaped onto a chandelier. When Marcella reached up to grab the cat from the light fixture, it jumped down and scratched her. As a consequence, Marcella developed cat scratch fever, which ultimately resulted in a debilitating stroke. She was paralyzed and confined to a wheelchair for the rest of her life. Iri did his best to look after Marcella and the young girls, but eventually a housekeeper, cook, and driver were employed to assist the family.

In December 1933, Iri parted ways with Messrs. Bishop and Vickery and founded his own printing and advertising company. Cope Incorporated was first located at 3800 Chester Avenue in the University Circle neighborhood of Cleveland. Bonne Bell, a cosmetics company founded in 1927 in Lakewood, Ohio, was a major customer of Iri's advertising coupons and circulars. Industrial customers such as General Tire, General Electric, and US Steel also enjoyed the mass appeal of sales catalogues printed by Cope.

By the end of the 1930s, Iri longed for a quiet place to take his family away from the bustle of the city, at least on weekends. Moreover, after Pearl Harbor, rumors were rampant that Axis bombers might target industrial cities such as Cleveland and Pittsburgh. "He wanted a safe place to take

Marcella Shupe (*Betty's mother, third from left*), at age six; her sister, Marion; father, Henry; and mother, Jeanette, circa 1909. *Henry family collection.*

Marcella and Iri Cope as newlyweds, circa 1923. *Henry family collection.*

Above: Betty Cope, age two, circa 1928. *Henry family collection.*

Left: Betty Cope, age one, at the family home in Shaker Heights, circa 1927. *Henry family collection.*

his family in case the world came to an end," Heidi Henry Cregar recalled. Always an avid outdoorsman, Iri purchased 130 acres of land in Bainbridge Township, Ohio, in 1942. Sensing another business opportunity, he began to raise black Angus cattle on the property. A small cabin was built for weekend stays, and a caretaker was hired to tend to the cattle.

In addition to his entrepreneurial efforts, Iri was a stockholder in Republic Steel of Cleveland; the Newton Steel Company of Trumbull County, Ohio; and other local companies. A member of the Cleveland Skating Club, Iri made a logical move in purchasing a stake in the Cleveland Barons AHL hockey team in the 1940s. A dedicated community supporter, he served on the Cleveland Chamber of Commerce and headed the local chapter of the American Cancer Society in 1948. He was an annual industrial donor to the Cleveland Community Fund, which was the precursor to the United Way.

Janet Cope (*left*), age four, and Betty Cope (*right*), age three, outside of their home in Shaker Heights, circa 1929. *Henry family collection.*

For her part, Marcella Cope, although wheelchair-bound, was also active in local civic and charitable organizations. She was highly involved in the service-oriented Cleveland Junior League and was a member of the board of the Amasa Stone House, which was a local healthcare facility for senior citizens. She adored Norwegian elkhounds and oversaw the breeding and raising of the dogs on the Bainbridge property. In frail health for most of her adult life, she died at the age of fifty-nine on March 28, 1965.

Iri Cope continued to manage the operation of his businesses for the remainder of his life. He died at the age of seventy on November 30, 1967. The strong spirit of adventure, entrepreneurship, and community-mindedness exemplified by her father indubitably motivated Betty Cope to embark on a career like no other.

2

Growing Up Cope

For the children of entrepreneur Iri Cope, growing up was a unique experience. The Copes fared better than many families during the Depression, mainly due to their father's strong business sense. Iri took a chance by starting his own printing and advertising business in 1933, but many customers from the previous partnership remained loyal to him, and the family survived.

However, their mother's early paralysis strained the family dynamics and ultimately shaped the daughters' personalities. Stroke victims in the 1930s had few resources for in-home therapy, and Marcella required much attention. Janet was the more emotionally sensitive of the two daughters and responded quickly to her mother's needs. Betty seemed to thrive on challenges, and naturally gravitated toward her entrepreneur father. While Betty always helped her mother when necessary, she couldn't wait for Iri to come home and took delight in reading her father's latest advertising brochures. By all accounts, Betty loved her mother but adored her father. According to Dr. Ellen Weber Libby, psychotherapist and author of *The Favorite Child*, it's common for children to feel closer to one parent rather than the other. "That doesn't mean that the child doesn't love both parents equally…It means that a given parent meets a given child's emotional needs in ways that are beyond words," stated Libby.

Despite their personality differences, Janet and Betty, who were born only sixteen months apart, were virtually inseparable. "Their mother's disability actually made them more independent and self-reliant," noted Heidi Henry

Betty, age six (*left*), and Janet, age seven (*right*), with Major, one of Marcella's Norwegian Elkhounds, circa 1932. *Henry family collection.*

Above: Betty Cope (*first row, fourth from left*) with her third-grade class at Shaker Heights elementary school, circa 1933. *Henry family collection.*

Right: Janet, age fourteen (*left*), and Betty, age thirteen (*right*), circa 1939. *Henry family collection.*

Cregar. Unlike mothers of other girls their age, Marcella couldn't take them on shopping trips to downtown department stores or to the theaters to see the latest movies. Heidi recalled, "Since their mother was confined to a wheelchair, they really had to be there for each other, and it made them closer. They were the greatest cheerleaders for each other all through their lives."

Both girls were excellent students at the Hathaway Brown School, a private, all-girls kindergarten through twelfth grade institution in Shaker Heights. In their eighth-grade years of 1938 and 1939, each sister and her HB friends traveled to Washington, D.C., a city that would play a significant role in Betty's later education. During their summer vacations, the girls attended the Cold Springs Camp for Girls in New York. The girls developed a love of horseback riding in summer camp, so Iri bought two horses for the girls to ride at the Bainbridge property.

Both Betty and Janet clearly displayed creativity and a natural flair for writing at an early age. "Iri encouraged them to use their imaginations," noted Janet's daughter KC Henry. Inspired by their father's printed brochures, the Cope daughters together created a monthly newsletter known as *Cope's Chronicle*, which Iri distributed free of charge to his customers and business contacts. Gathering statistics and trivia from Cleveland's three newspapers and some of Iri's publications, the girls prepared an entertaining circular. The 1940 issues contained important Ohio traffic safety data as well as amusing "light" news stories and fun facts about the number of teeth in a snail and rate of human hair growth.

The Cope daughters' love of writing was further manifested in plays that they wrote for family and friends. Like other girls growing up in the 1930s, Betty and Janet were captivated by radio dramas such as *Lux Radio Theater*, the *Mercury Theatre of the Air*, and *Inner Sanctum Mysteries*. In their high school years, Betty and Janet fervently wrote poetry and short stories for the HB literary journal, the *Specularia*. In 1943, Betty wrote a heartfelt poem from the viewpoint of a small boy who lost his father in the war.

Following in their mother's footsteps, both Janet and Betty engaged in community service. In the early 1940s, the sisters actively participated in wartime service projects, Janet in scrap drives and doll making for refugee children and Betty in welfare agency efforts. As a senior at HB, Betty was chairman of a school carnival to raise funds for the War Chest. Betty's goal was to raise $1,200, which was $200 over the previous year's carnival earnings. Community fundraising was clearly in her blood.

At age eighteen Janet and Betty each became debutantes and were introduced into society. Following graduation from HB in 1942,

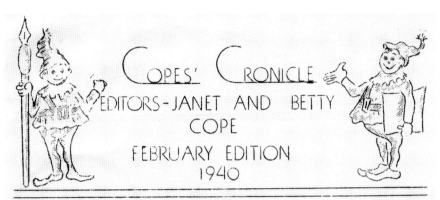

FINNS NEED OUR HELP

RIVER STREET LOSES DRINKWATER!

Everything's damp but his enthusiasm. And so Reuben Drinkwater, who lived on River street here, has moved to Coldwater to start a milk route.

*** *** *** *** *** ***

The longest telegram on record was a birthday greeting message sent to Pres. Franklin D. Roosevelt from Birmingham, Alabama, on January 30, 1934. This night letter, which required nineteen hours and eight minutes to send over high-speed automatic telegraph instruments, contained 41,000 signatures and it was a quarter of a mile in length.

*** *** *** *** *** ***

DID YOU KNOW THAT?---

Garlic has such a strong and permeating odor that it will flavor the milk of a cow that has only inhaled it for a few minutes.

That may be nice for the cow, but I wouldn't like the milk!

*** *** *** *** *** ***

THERE IS A CHANCE!

There are 11,000,000 unmarried women in the America and 15,000,000 unmarried men. We're certainly glad that it isn't the other way around. This being leap year, the figures probably will not be any wheres near the same by 1941, because it is also known that most dates are hinted at by the girl, and thus the girls will be popping the all important question.

WHO WILL HELP THE FINNISH SOLDIERS?

Will the Finns be helped? If so who will help them? Those are two important questions in Europe today. The English could help, the French could help and Americans could help. But the New World War is something that America wants to stay out of, that is in the fighting sense. But we can help. We can send money to the Finnish relief fund, or we can knit sweaters and send warm clothing to the Finnish soldiers.

Finland has stood up under the Russian attack remarkabley well and certainly we, the people of America, who live in this land of freedom can help another land in need.

*** *** *** *** ***

Above: Page 1 of the February 1940 edition of *Cope's Chronicle*, the newspaper written by Janet and Betty in their teenage years. *Henry family collection*.

Opposite: Page 2 of *Cope's Chronicle*, February 1940. *Henry family collection*.

EDITORIAL

Great were the things that he stood for,
Ever defending the right,
Often he rose for his country,
Ready and willing to fight.
Great were the deeds he accomplished,
Eagerly willing to give

Whatever he could for our freedom,
And striving that others might live.
So, as lands quarrel all 'round us,
Here let's remember that we,
In spite of the wars that are waging,
Now live in a land that is free.
Gaining that freedom's not easy,
The man who achieved it's not here,
Only, let's stop to salute him,
Now that his birthday is near.

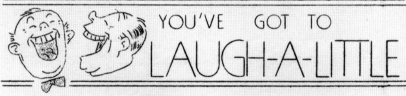

YOU'VE GOT TO LAUGH-A-LITTLE

HEARD BETWEEN THE EDITORS

Janet--If east is east and west is west, where's the twain?
Betty-On the twack.

******

Janet-I want a hot dog
Johnny-My feet are cold, too.

*****

Betty-You're so lazy.
Janet-How do you know? You've never seen me work.

*****

MOVIE MADNESS
(Dizzy Double Features)

"Blackmail" "The Old Maid"
"Mutiny in the Big House" "Fast and Furious"
"The Invisable Man returns" in "Invisable Stripes"
"Blondie Brings up Baby" "At the Balalika"

Confucius Say: Many Watts Make Light Work.

Above: Page 3 of *Cope's Chronicle*, February 1940. *Henry family collection.*

Opposite: Page 4 of *Cope's Chronicle*, February 1940. *Henry family collection.*

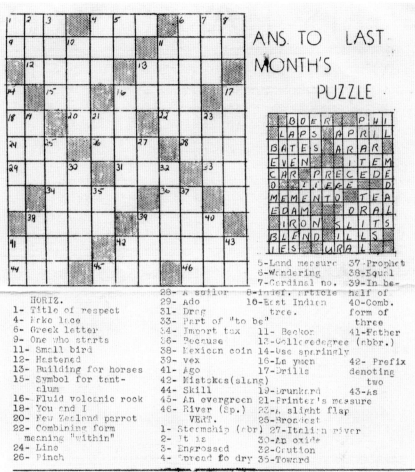

ANS. TO LAST MONTH'S PUZZLE

HORIZ.
1- Title of respect
4- Fake lace
6- Greek letter
9- One who starts
11- Small bird
12- Hastened
13- Building for horses
15- Symbol for tant-
    alum
16- Fluid volcanic rock
18- You and I
20- New Zealand parrot
22- Combining form
    meaning "within"
24- Line
26- Pinch

28- A sailor
29- Ado
31- Drag
33- Part of "to be"
34- Import tax
36- Because
38- Mexican coin
39- vex
41- Ago
42- Mistakes(slang)
44- Skill
45- An evergreen
46- River (Sp.)
   VERT.
1- Steamship (abbr)
2- It is
3- Engrossed
4- Spread to dry

5-Land measure
6-Wandering
7-Cardinal no.
8-indef. article
16-East Indian
   tree.
11- Beckon
13-Collegedegree (abbr.)
14-Use sparingly
16-La ymen
17-Drills
19-Drunkard
21-Printer's measure
23-A slight flap
25-Broadcast
27-Italian river
30-An oxide
32-Caution
35-Toward

37-Prophet
38-Equal
39-In be-
   half of
40-Comb.
   form of
   three
41-Father
42- Prefix
    denoting
    two
43-As

BE WELL DRESSED AND LOOK YOUR PART

W.B. DAVIS CLOTHES ARE SMART

(W.B. DAVIS SAY: NO LIKE CONFUCIUS)

STORE FOR MEN

Above: Betty (*left*) and Janet (*right*) modeling new swimsuits at the family home in Shaker Heights, circa 1942. *Henry family collection*.

Opposite: Betty Cope's senior photo (*at bottom*) in the Hathaway Brown School yearbook, 1943. *Henry family collection*.

Bard of rhyme and metre free —
Enjoy your dear wit —
Take the goods the gods provide thee —
Talk was like a stream —
You alone are you —

Elizabeth Cope

Janet entered Flora Stone Mather College in Cleveland. She fell in love with a young man and wanted to leave school to get married. Iri, the practical businessman who valued education more than romance, urged her to transfer to a school out of state. If she still felt the same way about her paramour after one year, he would allow her to leave school to marry him. Janet closed her eyes, ran her finger down a list of schools in a college directory and stopped at Hood College in Frederick, Maryland. Hood College it was!

In Betty's senior year, 1943, her writing skills, intelligence, talent, and independence were well documented by her peers who prepared the HB yearbook. Next to each senior photo was a poem in which the first letter of each stanza began with the letters in the person's name.

> *Bard of rhyme and metre free —*
> *Enjoy your dear wit —*
> *Take the goods the gods provide thee —*
> *Talk like a stream —*
> *You alone are you —*

There was never any doubt that after graduation from HB, Betty would go to college. She was passionate about writing and drama—why not combine these interests in her favorite medium, radio? Through a magazine advertisement, Betty learned about a radio dramatic arts program at Marjorie Webster Junior College in Washington, D.C. Radio drama was a unique major for an all-girls' college, and Betty seized the opportunity. Founded in 1920, the private institution offered liberal arts and business programs to traditional resident students as well as nonresident working students. With more women entering the workforce at the outbreak of World War II, the school provided practical programs of study for women, which appealed to Betty. The Webster School was also only fifty miles away from Hood College, so proximity to Janet might have been another factor in Betty's college decision-making process. She enrolled at Marjorie Webster in September 1943. As part of her curriculum, she most likely scripted dramas and produced programs for the school's radio station, WEBS.

Radio was an integral part of the lives of all Americans. By the mid-1930s, over two-thirds of American homes had radio sets. By the end of the decade, nearly 80 percent of Americans—about 25 million people—owned radios. The concept of writing programs and preparing them for broadcast to be heard by millions of people would enthrall a young writer like Betty.

Betty (*left*) as maid of honor at Janet's wedding to Fred Henry, 1946. *Henry family collection.*

The Marjorie Webster experience most likely shaped her mission in life—to inform and entertain.

Around this time, both Betty and Janet actively participated with other girls of their age in the Junior League of Cleveland, which assisted community agencies. They also raised thousands of dollars for the league through musical follies, which Betty produced. The follies were often broadcast on Cleveland's WGAR radio.

While Betty was consumed with college life, a few friends from her HB graduation class were getting married. Betty served as a dutiful bridesmaid for each of them. In the meantime, Janet graduated from Hood College. One summer during the postwar years, the sisters felt adventurous and rode their horses up Snake Hill, which lay across the Chagrin River from the cabin. They soon discovered that some boys who returned home from the war lived at the top of the hill. Naturally, Snake Hill became a popular place for them to exercise their horses.

Janet began seriously dating one returned veteran named Frederick Hawley Henry, whose family lived on Geauga Lake Road at the top of Snake Hill in Bainbridge. Fred graduated from Hiram College and held a distinguished service record as a B-17 pilot in Italy in World War II. On September 7, 1946, Janet and Fred were married at the First Baptist Church of Shaker Heights, with Betty filling the role of maid of honor.

While her sister and friends were planning their weddings, Betty was planning her own future in communications. For Betty, if marriage was meant to be, then it would come in due time. As she was absorbed with her writing, it didn't seem to matter much to her. While she was extremely happy for Janet, she remained focused on her own career goals. In the mid-1940s, however, local work as a radio drama writer was hard to find. Most Cleveland stations broadcast variety programs to showcase home-grown talent but relied on network feed for dramas. As Betty dreamed of selling scripts to the major networks, Iri employed her to write advertising copy for his company.

Nonetheless, for mass communication, the winds of change were blowing, and Betty would soon be caught up in them. Her ambition to work in the media landed her in the right place at exactly the right time.

3

The Girl with the TV Antenna Sticking Out of Her Head

One day in 1947, a client of Iri's visited the printing business, and Betty related the story of her plight to sell radio scripts. He suggested that she go into television. "Huh? What's that?" Betty responded.

FIRST IN OHIO

In July 1946, an FCC permit was granted to Scripps-Howard Radio Inc. for the construction of a television antenna. Scripps-Howard Inc. was the corporate father of the *Cleveland Press* newspaper. Jack Howard, the president of Scripps-Howard radio, spearheaded the effort to make television broadcasting an important part of their media service. The call letters for the Cleveland television station were to be WEWS, taken from E.W. Scripps's initials. It was a landmark move for the media company, since WEWS would be the first television station in Ohio and the sixteenth in the United States. Its studio was located at East Thirteenth Street and Chester Avenue in downtown Cleveland, in the heart of the theater district.

The ambitious would-be writer drove downtown in the summer of 1947 and filled out an application at the studio. She landed the job of station receptionist with no trouble. "Back in those days, receptionist or secretary was about the only off-camera job a woman would get at a TV station," said Fred Griffith, who later worked for Betty at WVIZ and became a program host at WEWS. As preparations were made for the station's first broadcast later that year, her role soon evolved to that of a "Girl Friday," assisting the manager and engineers wherever needed. WEWS first signed on the air as Channel 5 on December 17, 1947. Its first broadcast was the Cleveland Press Christmas pageant with special guest star Jimmy Stewart.

Early test pattern for WEWS, Channel 5, the first television station in Ohio, circa 1948. *WEWS archives.*

CHICAGO'S WIND BRINGS TALENT

"We're starting in the dark. This is brand new," wrote the "men of WEWS" in a 1947 Scripps-Howard Company newsletter. "There are no veterans in television." But there was one standout in the field who joined the station in January 1948. Jim Breslin was a World War II veteran who entertained troops and studied at the American Television Institute of Technology in Chicago. The institute provided instruction on the actual manufacture of television receivers as well as the production of television programs. Graduates of the institute earned bachelor of science degrees in television engineering. Breslin next taught television at Northwestern University and at the Goodman Theater. "It was such a new industry that we became experts in TV after one year," recalled Breslin. It was no wonder that the sixteenth station in the nation grabbed Breslin.

James Hanrahan, who worked for Scripps-Howard's radio division, was named the first manager of the station. Hanrahan quickly recognized Betty's intelligence and took a shine to her spunk. He encouraged her to shadow Breslin and learn as much as possible from him about the new medium. Breslin showed the young staff how to set up cameras, take long shots, and get close-ups. "Jim was like God since he had experience," Betty reflected on the fiftieth anniversary of WEWS in 1997.

Top: Betty Cope in the director's booth at WEWS, circa 1951.

Bottom: Betty Cope, circa 1953, directing live programs at WEWS. *CSU Memory Project*.

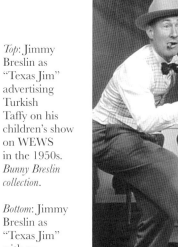

Top: Jimmy Breslin as "Texas Jim" advertising Turkish Taffy on his children's show on WEWS in the 1950s. *Bunny Breslin collection*.

Bottom: Jimmy Breslin as "Texas Jim" with an unidentified dancer on his children's show. *Bunny Breslin collection*.

Cleveland's Favorite Uncle

In 1948, Hanrahan gave Betty the task of directing the WEWS' live Children's Hour program known as *Uncle Jake's House*. Uncle Jake was the pseudonym for Gene Carroll, a veteran of Cleveland radio. Carroll and fellow performer Glenn Rowell created radio personalities "Jake and Lena." Uncle Jake's House consisted of an imaginary menagerie of animals plus a studio audience full of children under the age of ten. Uncle Jake would often call on audience members to perform. There was singing and dancing and lots of pretending. At the end of the program, children were told that they could "go downstairs in the elevator" to feed the animals in Uncle Jake's workshop. Thousands of Cleveland area kids couldn't wait to get on the show, just so that they could go for a ride in the elevator. In reality, the "elevator" consisted of a door, the upper half of which contained a large window. Away from the microphone, Director Betty instructed children to start bending their knees while standing behind the window, just to make it look like they were riding the elevator to the basement. One could imagine

Candy Lee Korn (*left*) with Gene Caroll as "Uncle Jake," Specs the cat and Clarence the dog, circa 1948. *Candy Lee Korn collection.*

Publicity photo of Candy Lee Korn on WEWS, circa 1952. *NE Ohio TV Memories.*

that the look of disappointment on the kids' faces as they left the studio rivaled that of learning the truth about Santa Claus or the Easter Bunny.

A few local children became regular performers on Uncle Jake's House, including Candy Lee Korn. Candy studied singing and dancing at a young age and, unlike many child stars, enjoyed her early experience on television. "I started performing on *Uncle Jake's House* on day one," recalled Candy. Birthday parties were standard fare at *Uncle Jake's House*, and it was Candy's job to assist with serving the cake and ice cream. Candy fondly remembers Betty as a calming presence on the set of *Uncle Jake's House*. "One day when I was serving ice cream to kids in the Peanut Gallery, I accidentally dropped a scoop on the back of a little girl's dress. Betty ran over in a flash and cleaned her up." As a young girl star on a live TV show, Candy noted, "I always felt comfortable knowing that Betty, as a woman, was there. She was so kind to us kids, but she really took charge of things."

SOMETHING FOR THE WOMAN OF THE HOUSE

Hanrahan must have felt that if Betty could handle Uncle Jake and the kids, she could tackle anything. She was next given the task of producing and directing *Distaff*, a Monday through Friday hour-long afternoon program aimed specifically at homemakers. During the postwar era, housewives comprised a large segment of the early afternoon television viewing audience. The *Akron Beacon-Journal* edition of February 13, 1949, raved about the program: "Using more sets than most Broadway plays, the program will look at the latest in cooking, fashions, shopping hints, decorating, and gardening. Viewers will see an ultra-modern kitchen, greenhouse, grocery store, style salon, living room, and office."

Betty assembled an all-star cast of local experts to present the various segments of *Distaff*. Alice Weston, a former newspaper women's page writer and Elyria mother of two, hosted the cooking segment; Ophelia Dudley Steed, a dietician at Western Reserve University spoke about family nutrition; Arnold Davis, director of the Cleveland Garden Center, discussed backyard flowers and vegetables; and Dorothy Fuldheim presented her own unique style of news analysis. The program also held contests for best recipes and floral arrangements. Betty's own creation was quite a class act for early local programming.

Perhaps the most memorable of Betty's discoveries for WEWS was Paige Palmer. Born Dorothy Rohrer, Paige graduated from Buchtel High School and attended the University of Akron. She taught fitness and dance classes at several local institutions but soon found that her ambitions lay far beyond the local scene. Paige entered and won the "Perfect Figure Contest" of 1942, which landed her a trip to New York City. There, she began hosting an early television show for women called *Fashion for Women and Their Homes*, sponsored by a large fabric company. By 1948, the New York show had ended, and Paige returned to northeast Ohio.

Right: Paige Palmer, fitness expert, exercising on her WEWS show directed by Betty, circa 1954. *Cleveland Classic Media Blog*.

Opposite, top: Unidentified delivery man (*left*), Alice Weston (*center*) and Ophelia Dudley Steed (*right*) on the set of the *Alice Weston Show*, which Betty directed on WEWS, circa 1948. *NE Ohio TV Memories*.

Opposite, bottom: Unidentified guest (*left*) and Alice Weston (*right*) prepare a meal on her WEWS program, which Betty directed, circa 1949. *NE Ohio TV Memories*.

The exact circumstances that brought Betty and Paige together have been lost to history, but clearly, they were kindred spirits. Like Betty, Paige was entrepreneurial and appreciated the value of education. At age sixteen, Paige rented a house in Akron and started her own "School of Expression" where she taught dance and encouraged friends to teach their music and crafts to others. Like her producer, Paige entered the business world shortly after completing college. As she was the former fashion editor of *Milady* magazine, taste and class were Paige's hallmarks, which appealed to Betty. The young producer hired Paige for a fifteen-week run at her own fitness show. Paige stayed on WEWS for the next twenty-five years.

In her trademark black leotard and fishnet stockings, Paige became a fixture in the homes of early WEWS viewers. Mothers of baby boomer children who needed to lose a few extra pounds tuned in to Paige's

WEWS publicity photo of Paige Palmer, who was also Cleveland's fashionista in the 1950s. *Author's collection.*

show and imitated her scissor-kicks, jumping jacks, and fanny bumps. Besides lecturing her viewers on nutrition, beauty, fitness and fashion, Paige encouraged housewives to turn their hobbies into businesses so that they might learn financial independence. She marketed exercise fashions under the Paige Palmer label and patented exercise equipment. After Paige's death in 2009, Betty reflected, "Paige was one of a kind. Somehow or another she invented herself and fit right into a new thing called television."

While Betty certainly had the knack for finding the talent for live TV, she also had to be versatile enough to substitute for the hosts when necessary. When Paige traveled to New York to survey the latest fashions, Betty, who kept herself physically fit, filled in admirably. When Rachael Van Cleve, another video cook on the *Mixing Bowl* program, suddenly took ill, Betty, who always enjoyed cooking, readily stepped in as a last-minute substitute. The resulting show became one of most memorable of Cleveland's early live television snafus.

First, Betty prepared the dry ingredients for a "hermit cookie" recipe, including flour, brown sugar, nuts. and raisins in one mixing bowl. The recipe called for three eggs. With her characteristic efficiency, she quickly proceeded to crack the eggs and pour their contents into a second mixing bowl. The only problem was that eggs were of an early vintage. "The second egg had an odor which paralyzed Betty's olfactory nerve ends," Stan Anderson of the *Cleveland Press* wryly noted. "It was easy to imagine it was brought into Ohio by the Connecticut men who pioneered this area." While the studio was filled with cries of disgust from nauseated cameramen and the floor crew, Betty calmly discarded the rotten eggs into a nearby garbage pail. Always the educator, Betty turned the episode into a lesson about checking the freshness of your ingredients. She later reached for some clean bowls, took some fresh eggs from the refrigerator and slowly cracked each one before proceeding with the mixing process.

These early live TV experiences thrilled Betty—combining her interest in live theater with her creative juices and resourcefulness. She frequently raved about this new career life to her friends and family. Around this time, close friend Edna Strnad arranged a blind date for Betty. Edna's future husband, Bud, brought home a fraternity brother on a holiday break. Betty and the frat brother double-dated with Edna and Bud. The next time that Bud brought his friend home for a visit, Edna tried again to pair him with Betty. The frat brother frantically backed off. "What? Not that girl with the TV antenna sticking out of her head!"

The Charm of the Announcer

Edna needn't have concerned herself with arranging dates for Betty, who was making plenty of social contacts through the broadcasting business. The most impressive of these was John Saunders. Born John Kocsany, he was raised on Cleveland's East Side, graduated from John Adams High School, attended the School of Speech at Northwestern University and obtained an associate's degree in political science and public administration from Miami University. John worked for five years as a radio announcer and reporter for WGAR before moving on to a program director position at a rival station further up the dial, WERE. The handsome announcer acted in local productions at Cain Park Theater and received rave reviews for his portrayal of Woodrow Wilson in Howard Koch and John Huston's *In Time to Come*. He was also civic-minded, even running unsuccessfully for Cleveland City Council in 1947.

With his deep announcer's voice, the role John liked best was playing Santa Claus for local parties. John repeated his role for a 1948 children's Christmas broadcast at WEWS, and Betty was quickly smitten. By January 1950, they were engaged. Significantly, Betty chose Iri's birthday, Monday, July 24, 1950, as her wedding date. Betty and John tied the knot amid elegant candelabras, bouquets of daisies and delphiniums and Italian lace tablecloths at her parents' Moreland Courts apartment in Shaker Heights. Dr. Harold Cooke Phillips of the First Baptist Church officiated, while Janet served as maid of honor, and Crandall Hendershott, studio organist at WEWS, provided musical accompaniment. The newlyweds resided in an apartment on Kemper Road in Shaker Heights.

She Must Not Disappoint the Children

Thanksgiving weekend of 1950 proved to be the most memorable holiday of Betty's television career. Thanksgiving Day temperatures hovered around forty degrees; however, it dropped rapidly overnight due to the unexpected passage of an arctic air mass. On Friday, November 24, one of the greatest blizzards in U.S. history struck Ohio and the Appalachian region. By Saturday, over twenty-two inches of snow had fallen in Cleveland. The airport closed, and over ten thousand abandoned cars blocked the city streets. Mayor Thomas Burke declared a state of emergency, called for the

John Saunders (*left*) and Betty (*right*) at their July 1950 wedding in her parents' home. *Henry family collection.*

National Guard, mobilized snow removal equipment to clear the snow, and banned nonessential cars from downtown Cleveland.

Betty was scheduled to direct the children's Christmas show on WEWS on Saturday, November 25. It was going to be Cleveland's first 1950 telecast to feature Santa, played by none other than John Saunders. However, the snowstorm had buried the city, and all auto travel was banned. Buses and trolleys were few and far between.

But Betty was determined. She knew how popular the children's shows had become, and she just couldn't disappoint the audience. "How do you tell the kids Santa Claus isn't going to make it in a snowstorm?" she later said. Betty was a keen horseback rider on the cabin grounds in Bainbridge, so she would make her skills pay off. She called a riding academy near her Shaker Square home and rented a horse. Betty and John saddled up and rode from Shaker Boulevard to East Thirteenth Street in downtown Cleveland. They made it to the station in plenty of time for the party.

The local press viewed Betty as more of a novelty than a dedicated director. Following the storm, Beatrice Vincent of the *Cleveland Press* wrote, "For the next couple of days, Betty Cope, one of the few women directors in the country, was also one of the few directors to go about her chores in slacks and a sweater. No one seemed to mind, however. With the big blizzard of 1950 keeping them close to home, they were too happy to see their favorite TV programs coming up on schedule to wonder about the apparel of the persons directing them." Vincent continued, "Like her male counterparts, Betty spends most of her time in script conferences, patiently rehearsing shows before they go on the air, hunting ideas for new ones, [and] designing civic programs. Hours are long and directors must be flexible."

"I AM the Director!"

Betty's determination to succeed in television saw her through discriminating situations. While planning a broadcast from Cleveland for *The Toast of the Town*, which was later known as *The Ed Sullivan Show*, a director from CBS in New York called WEWS to confirm the arrangements for the direct feed. Betty answered the phone call. "Let me talk to the director," boomed the CBS rep. "I AM the director," Betty answered calmly. There was a long pause on the other end of the phone.

At CBS, word caught on that its Cleveland affiliate employed a female director. Indeed, in the 1950s, a woman in television production was considered a curiosity or perhaps even an eccentricity. In 1953, Mark Goodson and Bill Todman, the producers of *What's My Line*, invited Betty to appear as a guest. Betty stumped the panel, which included Steve Allen, who had forgotten that he had met Betty in 1950 during a Cleveland Heart Fund telethon.

WEWS: THE CLEVELAND SCHOOL OF TELEVISION

Under the direction of James Hanrahan, WEWS became the breeding ground for Cleveland's early television groundbreakers. Besides Betty Cope and Jimmy Breslin, Hanrahan also hired Jack Moffitt, who first came to the station as a page the day before it opened in 1947. After a stint in the army, he rose to the station's public service director and promotions director. Moffitt covered the Algerian war for the station. He also produced some of Dorothy Fuldheim's programs. Later, Moffit became the manager of Cleveland's first major independent commercial UHF station, WUAB. Moffitt turned the station into one of the largest-reaching UHF stations in the Midwest.

In addition to hiring one of the first female directors, Hanrahan also hired the first Black man, George Moore, as director. Moore worked as investigative reporter and columnist at the *Cleveland Press* until 1947, when Hanrahan offered him a directing job. George Moore became a charter employee of WEWS. Bill Weidenmann joined Hanrahan's team at WEWS in January 1948. He worked as an expert cameraman at the Indians' and Browns' games as well as the PGA Tour. Nicknamed "Dad," Weidenmann went on to direct WEWS's *Morning Exchange* program for two decades. In a 1997 *Plain Dealer* article celebrating the fiftieth anniversary of WEWS and its legendary early crew, Betty recalled that station manager Hanrahan "was a visionary and brilliant man."

If WMAQ in Chicago with its "graduates" Dave Garroway, Burr Tillstrom, and Fran Allison was known as the "Chicago School of Television," then WEWS was Cleveland's School of Television. Its graduates—James Hanrahan, Betty Cope, Dorothy Fuldheim, Jimmy Breslin, Jack Moffitt, Paige Palmer, Alice Weston, and Bill Wiedenmann—were the true television pioneers of Cleveland.

Through it all, Betty did not consider herself a trailblazer. She was given a job, and she wanted to get the job done completely and correctly. Betty Cope simply wanted to present quality television programs to her beloved Cleveland audience.

The years 1954 and 1955 would bring personal and professional changes and challenges for Betty and WEWS. As always, the girl with the TV antenna sticking out of her head would rise to the occasion.

4

Necessity Is the Mother of Captain Penny

Betty was a whirlwind," recalled Bunny Breslin, daughter of WEWS's Jimmy Breslin, who often visited her father during his early years at the station. "She was like a top, always spinning with so much energy around the studio." Indeed, directing three live shows per day, five days per week, kept Betty on her toes. Preparation of the shows was even more time consuming: her days were filled with such tasks as reviewing program logs and scripts, inviting guests, and rehearsing the shows, ensuring that programs were kept within time constraints. "As a director in those days, you had to do everything from writing the scripts to calling the shots from the control room," remembered Breslin. "You had to know where the cameras would be placed, at which angles, in which directions, with which lighting, and know what to show the audience." Moreover, the producer-directors' job required much office work; there were phone calls to be made to sponsors and networks. As a consequence, Betty practically lived at the East Thirteenth Street studio. She was meticulous; she put her whole heart and soul into every production. But there was satisfaction in knowing that she produced and directed quality shows for Clevelanders.

From her childhood days through her college years, Betty thrived on challenges. The atmosphere of live television production was both thrilling and exhausting for Betty. Her relationship with her husband, however, was becoming more strained. Outside observers cannot know all the factors that influence relationships between husbands and wives. But by all accounts, Betty and John parted amicably. Saunders left Cleveland for Detroit to take a position as TV expert with the advertising firm of MacManus, John, and Adams. In 1955, the *Cleveland Plain Dealer* reported that the veteran Cleveland Santa performer was now "in charge of Kris Kringle programming for 10 cities for the S.S. Kresge Co."

As a much-needed change of scenery, Betty planned a European vacation. In early April 1954, a *Plain Dealer* society page article announced that Betty

Ron Penfound, a.k.a. "Captain Penny," whom Betty chose to host an afternoon children's show in 1955. *Author's collection.*

would set sail on the luxury liner *United States* for Europe on Saturday, April 10. Janet and Fred drove her to New York and saw her off the pier. Betty spent eight weeks of the spring of 1954 traveling in England, France, Germany, Italy, and Switzerland. During her return trip on the same vessel, Betty met and had several talks with Haile Selassie, emperor of Ethiopia. After traveling by steamship, rowboat, motorboat, and subway, the only unpleasant moment of her trip occurred when she became airsick on the flight from New York, fifteen minutes before the plane landed in Cleveland. During her vacation, cameraman Al Herrick filled in admirably as director on *Uncle Jake's House* and other programs.

Since late 1947, WEWS had been the CBS mainstay. Through 1948, WEWS intermittently carried some Dumont and NBC programming. NBC had found its permanent northeast Ohio home at WNBK, which first signed on the air on October 31, 1948. Broadcasting on VHF Channel 4, it was the fourth of NBC's five original owned-and-operated stations to sign on, three weeks after WNBQ (now WMAQ-TV) in Chicago. WXEL became the last of Cleveland's three VHF television stations when it signed on as Channel 9 as WXEL on December 17, 1949. Built by the Empire Coil Co. of New Rochelle, New York, the station originally occupied quarters at Pleasant Valley and State Roads in Parma and carried primarily DuMont programs. An FCC-ordered realignment of VHF channels in the Midwest forced WXEL to move to Channel 8 on December 10, 1953; WNBK shifted to Channel 3 in April 1954.

By the mid-1950s, the Cleveland television scene was quickly changing. In 1954, Empire Coil sold two of its television interests—WXEL and KPTV in Portland, Oregon, the United States' first UHF station—to Storer Broadcasting. George B. Storer, the company's founder and president, was a member of the board of directors of CBS and used his influence to take the CBS television affiliation from WEWS in March 1955. WEWS had no choice but to accept ABC affiliation, since the DuMont network shut down operations in 1955. WEWS was also an affiliate of the short-lived Paramount Television Network. The station was one of the network's strongest affiliates, airing such Paramount programs as *Time for Beany*. Finding it impossible to battle against the CBS and NBC giants, Paramount ceased its network operation in 1956.

The switch to ABC was nothing short of a dilemma for WEWS producers. Compared to CBS, the "Third Network" offered little in the way of daytime programming. While CBS broadcast such soap opera hits as *The Guiding Light* and *As the World Turns* each afternoon, ABC

It takes a load of adjectives to tell about Cleveland's most modern television plant, the brand-new, ultra-modern, giant-size WEWS. Here are Ohio's best-and-biggest studios. And that goes for WEWS shows and person-alities, too. Ask Blair-TV.

WEWS trade advertisement touting its new studios in 1956. *NE Ohio TV Memories*.

offered—well—nothing. Faced with an empty afternoon program slate, Betty's creative juices started flowing. Trains were forever popular toys with kids; why not create a kids' show with a train engineer? Elyria native Ron Penfound was an announcer and sportscaster-wannabe at WEWS. In March 1955, Betty put a train engineer's hat on the handsome twenty-eight-year-old Penfound's head, nicknamed him "Captain Penny," and awarded him the job of hosting a children's program. *The Captain Penny Show* featured Little Rascals and Three Stooges shorts along with old cartoons. Live characters, including Earl Keyes (Mr. Jingleling and Wilbur Wiffenpoof), also turned up on the show. Once a week, Captain Penny presented animals that were available for adoption through the Cleveland Animal Protective League. At the close of each daily show, Captain Penny advised his young audience, "You can fool some of the people all of the time, all of the people some of the time, but you can't fool Mom. She's pretty nice and she's pretty smart. Do what Mom says, and you won't go far wrong." *The Captain Penny Show* was a favorite with Cleveland-area kids for the next sixteen years.

Out of necessity, more local creativity permeated the Channel 5 studios in the mid-1950s. Producer-director Jimmy Breslin started his own afternoon children's show on Channel 5. Drawing on his Chicago Institute of Television experience, he entertained kids with his cowboy character "Texas Jim" and the absentminded "Professor Ewell Flunk."

To fill in the morning hours, Betty herself went in front of the cameras as hostess of the *Channel 5 Morning Movie*. Always a fan of classic dramas and musicals, she provided knowledgeable background and commentary on the films. In 1956, *Cleveland Plain Dealer* TV critic Tom O'Connell praised Betty as doing a "smooth and professional job" presenting the movies.

As more local programs were being produced, WEWS found that it had outgrown its East Thirteenth Street studios. The station moved to a more modern studio on the corner of East Thirtieth Street and Euclid Avenue on the outskirts of downtown Cleveland late December 1956.

Dorothy Fuldheim had been a fixture at WEWS since its inception in 1947. She anchored its first local newscast and later hosted her own evening news program, interviewing public figures and providing intriguing, insightful commentaries. In 1957, Betty chose to draw on Dorothy's talent for an early afternoon program. She teamed Dorothy with local radio personality Bill "Smoochie" Gordon to co-host the *One O'Clock Club*, a variety and talk show aimed at housewives. It was the first program broadcast from the new studios, and it was a gem. Dorothy's

fiery personality and Gordon's wild and crazy sense of humor resulted in volatile yet entertaining conversations. Produced by Betty and directed by Jimmy Breslin, the show featured a live band and interviews with guest stars such as Bob Hope and a young Frankie Avalon. For $1.50, the public could gain admission to the studio, have a pre-show luncheon, and sit in the audience for the program.

WEWS's local shows of the 1950s proved immensely popular with both children and adults. "Those were the fun years," remarked Bunny Breslin. "Both Betty and Dad were made for their jobs. They had the freedom to shoot from the hip. The local shows were the lifeblood of the station. It was like a local theater or improv group, full of bloopers."

In addition to its local popularity, there were kudos for WEWS on a national level. In particular, Betty and Dorothy's achievements were recognized in a 1956 ABC Sunday afternoon program titled *Tomorrow's Careers: Women in Radio and Television*, which was an offshoot of the *Johns Hopkins Science Review*. Dorothy Lewis, radio and television coordinator for station relations of the UN, effused, "I wish you could see and meet Miss Betty Cope who began in blue jeans as a matter of fact as floor manager and today is the program manager of this fine station. And women really have a chance in Cleveland—here's Cleveland's globetrotting grandmother—

Above: Dorothy Fuldheim interviewing Dr. Walter Alvarez, physician and medical journalist, on her WEWS talk show. *Author's collection*.

Right: Betty teamed Cleveland radio host Bill Gordon (shown here in 1955) with Dorothy Fuldheim for the *One O'Clock Club* show on WEWS in the 1950s. *NE Ohio TV Memories*.

Opposite: Dorothy Fuldheim interviewing Cleveland mayor Ralph Perk and *Plain Dealer* editor Thomas Vail on her Channel 5 program. *Author's collection*.

Dorothy Fuldheim," as footage of the world-renowned reporter's on-site interviews was shown.

By 1956, however, the atmosphere at WEWS was changing. "There was a perceptible shift in philosophy," remembered Breslin. "Dad and the other producers felt a great deal of pressure to keep the bottom line as low as possible." The station had just moved to the huge new studio, and increasingly sophisticated and expensive equipment had been purchased. Extended programming hours meant rising broadcasting costs, and the push was on to find additional sponsors.

But it was more than just the financial picture that was changing. There was an evolution in the nature of the TV audience, and this had an impact on the type of programming that was shown. The medium's early days, known as the "Golden Age of Television," introduced original live anthology drama series, many of which received critical acclaim. Examples of these shows included CBS's *Playhouse 90* and *Westinghouse Studio One* and NBC's *Kraft Television Theatre* and the *Philco Television Playhouse*. Commercial network television was dominated by high culture programming in the 1950s with live classical concerts and reenactments of Broadway performances on the *Bell Telephone Hour*. Programming

Advertising man Robert Evans (*left*) became Betty's second husband in 1959. *Henry family collection.*

concepts were innovative, and they showcased tremendous writing talents.

In 1950, the price of a TV set was the equivalent of several weeks' salary for the average American worker. Most of the audience consisted of Northeast and Midwest urban residents who lived within reception range of the major stations. The programs broadcast at this time simply mirrored the demographics. By 1956, TV sets had become less expensive and hundreds of new stations opened across the country. At the beginning of the decade, only 9 percent of U.S. households owned television sets. By 1959, that figure had increased to nearly 86 percent. Television signals began reaching more rural communities. The nature of TV programming changed to reflect the tastes of this ever-growing, diversified audience. Filmed westerns and conventional American family situation comedies began to rule the airwaves. This trend continued until the advent of the cultural and social revolutions of the late 1960s.

All the while, ABC was the bottom rung of this three-step ladder. From 1950 to 1955, the only ABC show to break the Nielsen top 10 was *Disneyland*. Housewives and kids regularly tuned to Channel 5 local shows in the afternoons. But by evening, families usually switched to Channels 3 or 8. This perception as the "Third Network" affiliate did not sit well with WEWS management.

The pressure for high ratings and cost containment seemed to take the fun out of the adventure of early TV broadcasting. There had to be something more to television, and Betty was reaching for it.

By the close of the decade, there was a change in the direction of Betty's personal life as well. On Valentine's Day 1959, Betty embarked on her second marriage, this time to a local advertising man by the name of Robert Evans. The wedding, which was kept to a small crowd of family and friends, was held at the Shaker Heights Country Club. The Reverend Russell Bishop of the First Baptist Church officiated, and Janet Henry again served as maid of honor. Betty and Bob Evans honeymooned in Key West and settled in an apartment on Euclid Heights Boulevard in Cleveland Heights.

Given the changes at WEWS and her home life, Betty began to give serious thought to a career change. With her background in advertising and television production and connections with local politicians through the station newsroom, she decided to create her own business of producing political advertisements. The commencement of her new enterprise would coincide with President John F. Kennedy's "New Frontier" of 1961.

In December 1960, Betty produced one of the most ambitious programs of her television career. Simulcast by WDOK radio and sponsored by the Illuminating Company, *Moments of Christmas* featured music from the Cleveland Orchestra, professional singers and dancers and church choirs and included nine vignettes of the story of Christmas. It was truly a spectacular way for Betty to finish her career at WEWS.

5

A Cleveland Epic

The Birth of a Station

The story of the birth of Betty Cope's beloved Channel 25 is as amazing a tale as any D.W. Griffith epic. It began unobtrusively, but as the years went by, high drama ensued. Fraught with warring factions, misconceptions, suspicions, undying devotion, unshakable determination and, finally, success, it is entertaining from the beginning to the present day.

In the Beginning: A First for Cleveland

Let us start with a little-known fact: educational broadcasting actually got its start in Cleveland. Though it's not the channel you might be thinking of, this local station was something of a historic landmark in the regular transmission of educational programming.

In 1925, representatives from college- and university-owned radio stations met in Washington, D.C., and formed the Association of College and University Broadcasting Stations. Their goals were to seek channel reservations and find a means of exchanging programs. Their membership was low, and their budget practically nonexistent. They regrouped in 1934 to form the National Association of Educational Broadcasters (NAEB). Congress passed the Communications Act of 1934, which established the Federal Communications Commission (FCC) to regulate interstate and international communications by wire and radio. Through the FCC,

.C.C. Form No. 452

UNITED STATES OF AMERICA
FEDERAL COMMUNICATIONS COMMISSION

RADIO STATION LICENSE

File no. B2-LED-1
Official No. 1
Call letters W B O E

ION-COMMERCIAL EDUCATIONAL BROADCAST .... BROADCAST ....
(Class of station) .... (Nature of service)

2415 Abell Avenue, Cleveland, Ohio .... Lat. 41° 28' 05" North,
(Location of station) .... Long. 81° 35' 40" West.

Subject to the provisions of the Communications Act of 1934, subsequent acts, and treaties, and all regulations heretofor
r hereafter made by this Commission, and further subject to the conditions and requirements set forth in this license, th
.ICENSEE, CLEVELAND CITY BOARD OF EDUCATION, CHARLES H. LAKE, SUPERINTENDENT
s hereby authorized to use and operate the radio transmitting apparatus, hereinafter described, for radio communication for th
erm beginning November 21 ...., 1938, and ending April 1 ...., 193 9
(F.m. Eastern standard time) .... (3 a.m. Eastern standard time)

1. (a) On the following frequencies (in kc): 41500 kilocycles

   (b) Types of emission: A-3

   (c) The frequency must be maintained within the tolerance limits specified in column 7 of paragraph 5.
2. With an output power not in excess of 500 watts.
3. To communicate as a non-commercial educational broadcast station in
   accordance with Rules 1050, 1057, 1058 and 1059.

4. Hours of service: Unlimited.
5. Apparatus authorized to be used is described as follows:

1 MANUFACTURER	2 TYPE	3 SERIAL NO.	4 RATED POWER (WATTS)	5 EMISSION	6 FREQUENCY RANGE (KC)	7 TOLERANCE PER CENT
Collins	236-A	–	500	A-3		0.01

Painting and Lighting of the antenna system not required at the present time,
provided however, that nothing contained herein shall be construed as a finding by
the Commission on the question of marking or lighting of the antenna system should
future conditions require. Licensee expressly agrees to install such marking or
lighting as the Commission may hereafter require, under the provisions of Section 3
of the Communications Act of 1934.

This license is issued on the licensee's representation that the statements contained in licensee's application are true and
hat the undertakings therein contained, so far as they are consistent herewith, will be carried out in good faith. The license
hall, during the term of this license, render such service as will serve public interest, convenience, or necessity to the full exten
f the privileges herein conferred.

This license shall not vest in the licensee any right to operate the station nor any right in the use of the frequencies desig
ated in the license beyond the term hereof, nor in any other manner than authorized herein. Neither the license nor the righ
ranted hereunder shall be assigned or otherwise transferred in violation of the Communications Act of 1934. This license i
ubject to the right of use or control by the Government of the United States conferred by section 606 of the Communication
ct of 1934.

Dated this 21st .... day of November ...., 193 8

By DIRECTION OF THE FEDERAL COMMUNICATIONS COMMISSION,

[SEAL]

U. S. GOVERNMENT PRINTING OFFICE   16—397   Secretary.

FCC license for WBOE, the nation's first educational radio station, located in Cleveland,
1938. *CMSD archives.*

broadcasting would now follow a more orderly path to development. The NAEB began to pressure the FCC to reserve frequencies for educational broadcasting. After four years of lobbying, their efforts finally paid off. In January 1938, the FCC agreed to issue licenses to nonprofit educational organizations provided they broadcast at higher frequencies than commercial stations. The Cleveland Board of Education soon applied for and received a construction permit to build a radio station for the sole purpose of broadcasting educational programs to its schools. On November 21, 1938, the FCC granted a license to WBOE, whose call letters were derived from the Board of Education. Thus, Cleveland could boast the first authorized educational broadcasting station.

WBOE's facilities were originally located in the Lafayette School on Abell Avenue. Later, the station moved to the sixth floor of the Board of Education Building on East Sixth Street. Its transmitting frequency was much higher than standard radios could tune to at this time. As a consequence, 150 specially constructed receivers were purchased and distributed to the various city schools. By 1939, WBOE was broadcasting instructional material for students from kindergarten through high school weekdays from 8:30 a.m. to 4:30 p.m. Lessons in subjects such as history, science, arithmetic, geography, spelling, and safety were sent into classrooms

Lobby of WBOE educational radio station in Cleveland. *CMSD archives.*

Top: Master control room at WBOE educational radio station. *CMSD archives*.

Bottom: Receivers such as the one shown at right were required for classroom reception of WBOE radio programs. *CMSD archives*.

Top: Cleveland school students rehearsed a play for broadcast at WBOE, circa 1940. *CMSD archives*.

Bottom: Educational programs were recorded on wax disks at WBOE. *CMSD archives*.

each day. The station shipped corresponding work sheets to students and lesson guides to teachers. Broadcast material was often synchronized with film strips or slides to add a visual dimension to the lessons and heighten students' interest levels.

In 1940, the FCC chose to eliminate broadcasting at the higher frequency levels and authorized the use of FM bands, which offered improved sound quality. WBOE eventually moved to 90.1 and later 90.3 MHz. By the 1960s, WBOE was broadcasting more general-interest programs on music and drama. The station struggled financially and eventually ceased operations in 1978.

The essential need for a separate broadcasting channel for education was proclaimed by H.M. Buckley, assistant superintendent of Cleveland Public Schools in 1938. "We should make clear the distinction between educational and commercial broadcasting, thereby eliminating the conflict due to the use of a common measuring-stick for educational and commercial programs," noted Buckley. His words would ring true for the next generation of broadcasting media as well.

Radio Was Great, But Now It's Out of Date

Other cities such as New York, Chicago, and Minneapolis followed Cleveland's lead and started their own educational radio stations. For many communities, however, the costs of educational broadcasting proved to be prohibitive. Moreover, FM receivers in the 1940s were few and far between. By the end of World War II, the focus of broadcasting had shifted to an entirely new horizon. In 1948, television had expanded so greatly across the United States that the number of stations threatened to exceed the twelve very high frequency (VHF) outlets that were allotted by the FCC. Overwhelmed by applications for new stations, the FCC deferred all activity so that it could conduct hearings to investigate the expansion of television broadcasting into the ultrahigh frequency (UHF) range. During these hearings, the NAEB again lobbied for channels to be reserved for educational purposes. Around the time that the hearings concluded in 1951, the Ford Foundation created the Fund for the Advancement of Education and the Fund for Adult Education. The foundation donated $90,000 to the Joint Committee on Educational Television (which included the NAEB and the National Education Association) to assist with legal fees in its push for TV station allocations.

In 1952, the FCC lifted its freeze on television station allotments. Of its 2,053 allocations, 242 or 12 percent were reserved for noncommercial purposes. The reservations consisted of 162 UHF and 80 VHF stations. An ambitious faculty group at the University of Houston used an oil industry grant to launch KUHT as the nation's first noncommercial educational television (ETV) station in 1953. In Pittsburgh, Leland Hazard, corporate attorney and vice-president of the Pittsburgh Plate Glass Company (PPG), spearheaded the movement toward creating educational television station WQED. Along with the Mellon Foundation and Westinghouse Electric, PPG financed the equipment and facilities for the station. For his part, Hazard took a unique step to obtain operational funds for the station: he called on the community to donate to WQED. About 8 percent of Western Pennsylvania's TV set owners and half of its area school districts did make those contributions, and on April 1, 1954, WQED took to the air. Labor costs were kept low at the station as high school and college students with an interest in broadcasting volunteered behind the scenes.

Dr. Burr Roney teaches a biology class on KUHT, the nation's first educational television station at the University of Houston, circa 1953. *University of Houston archives.*

TV IS THE THING...THIS YEAR?

While the road to broadcasting educational radio in Cleveland was a smooth one, the path to launching Cleveland's educational television station was far rockier. As early as June 1951, Cleveland Public Library, the Cleveland Board of Education, and Western Reserve University expressed great interest in applying for a permit for a joint educational UHF television station. The concept of learning through the new medium seemed to be quite popular in the city. By the fall of that year, WEWS partnered with John Carroll University, Western Reserve University (WRU, precursor to Case Western Reserve University) and the University of Akron to offer weekday morning televised courses on such subjects as psychology, geography, literature, and music appreciation to students. The broadcasts were funded by the Cleveland Foundation and seven anonymous private citizens. John F. White, vice-president of WRU, reported the following spring that "telecourses" broadcast on commercial television were extremely successful, with 1,250 paying students. In fact, White noted, the test scores of students watching from home were an average of 13 points higher than those of campus-based students. White further indicated that telecourses were popular among Cleveland's elderly as well as veterans recovering at Crile Hospital. James Hanrahan, general manager of WEWS, referred to the telecourse students as "bright feathers in our cap."

John H. White, vice-president of Western Reserve University in Cleveland and later president of National Educational Television. *Author's collection.*

While the concept of offering education through a commercial station was a noble one, the Board of Education was concerned about just that...working through the outlet of commercial station. Their concern was that commercial advertising dollars might dictate the nature of the programming that was intended for educational purposes. A publicly funded television station, they felt, was the most objective

Mark C. Schinnerer, superintendent of Cleveland Public Schools in the 1950s and '60s and proponent of educational television. *Author's collection.*

means of transmitting instructional programs. The public should fund the media outlet through which its children should be educated.

By this time, the FCC had reserved Channel 25 for Cleveland's educational purposes. While the Cleveland Public Schools and the Board of Education signed a letter of intent to the FCC for the broadcast rights to this station, no formal license application was made. Mark C. Schinnerer, superintendent of Cleveland Public Schools, made it clear that "we in no way will be entering into competition with commercial stations. We will not be aiming at mass audiences, but small groups." In March 1953, the school board took the superintendent's suggestion and voted to appropriate $500,000 for an educational television station.

Meanwhile, Cleveland's local universities were quite content with the prospect of continuing to broadcast classes on the commercial stations and saw no need to push for educational TV. The FCC's deadline for filing the application for Channel 25 was June 2, 1953. WRU's White pledged "continued cooperation with commercial stations as well as with any education television channel or network which might be put into effect here." However, universities in various other parts of Ohio were thinking otherwise: Ohio State University, Kent State, Miami, Bowling Green, and Ohio University were reportedly exploring a statewide noncommercial TV educational network.

Realizing the lack of available funds and UHF transmitters, Cleveland school board superintendent Schinnerer did a complete about-face. In April 1953, he tried to put the brakes on a proposal for building an educational TV station, mainly in the hopes that a possible delay might encourage more public interest and financial contributions. School board members nonetheless proceeded with plans to hire a radio-television engineer, Carl Smith, to survey options to build the station for the school district. Smith submitted a recommendation to construct, equip, and operate the station for approximately $574,000.

MAJOR MISCONCEPTIONS
AND THE DREAM LIES DORMANT

But there were pressures from underpaid teachers for higher salaries and a sense of apprehension on the part of teachers who feared that television would replace their jobs. There was complete unfamiliarity with the new medium in the educational realm. Furthermore, there was a great need for new school buildings to place the growing baby boomer population. Amid much insecurity and in-fighting, the school board put the entire project on ice.

June 2, 1953, came and went, but no license application for an educational station was filed. By September of that year, *Plain Dealer* (PD) TV critic George Condon declared the project dead. "When that body [the Board of Education], in the face of public apathy, decided to hold the TV project in abeyance, the initial enthusiasm generated by its proponents was dissipated and virtually nothing has been heard about it since." Condon went on to describe Pittsburgh's success in raising funds for educational broadcasting through the industrial and public sectors, noting, "Maybe educators and civic leaders in this area could learn a lesson or two in the Pittsburgh school."

CITIZENS UNITE AND APPEAL TO CONGRESS

Discussions about educational television continued among a nucleus of interested educators and business leaders for the next few years. In 1958, this group organized formally as the Greater Cleveland Television Education Association (GCTEA). The association was comprised of representatives from northeast Ohio schools, universities, museums, libraries, and industries. It organized as a corporation in the spring of 1959. The primary goal of the GCTEA was to activate Channel 25 through coordination of information from local, state, and national resources; educating the public about the station; and raising funds to equip and staff the station from foundations, individuals, and industry.

The association spent months talking to experts in the engineering field regarding the pros and cons of UHF versus VHF and came to the conclusion that it made more sense to use the already available UHF outlet of Channel 25 rather than wait possibly years for the FCC to grant another VHF outlet to Cleveland. The association traveled to New York to meet with the head of the National Education Television Center, John F. White (formerly vice-president of WRU), to seek direction and advice for planning station operation. Locally, they opened board meetings to the public to keep them informed of their progress.

The GCTEA also brought engineering consultants to Cleveland to discuss the necessary equipment and personnel and to help choose the most appropriate site for the station. Around 1960, KYW (formerly WNBK), Cleveland's NBC affiliate, vacated their first studio at 815 Superior Avenue for a new facility at East Sixth Street and Rockwell Avenue. KYW offered its old studio, outdated equipment and all, to the GCTEA rent-free for the first six months. In taking many investigative initial steps, the GCTEA announced that it was ready to launch Channel 25 but needed citizen interest and financial support.

The U.S. Senate announced the introduction of S.B. 205 in 1960, which, if passed, would provide much-needed funding for (then) state-of-the-art equipment for educational television stations. Upon learning of this proposed legislation, the GCTEA rushed to Washington to present a statement in support of the bill before Congress, a portion of which follows:

> *If the GCTEA, incorporated in 1959, had its way, it would have had Channel 25 on the air tomorrow. It is an embarrassment that Cleveland is the last place in Ohio, and nearly the last metropolitan area in the United States without ETV for its schools and for other educational uses.*
>
> *It is not the time to point the finger, review the past, and bemoan why do we not have ETV here today. It is more constructive to tell the Cleveland public what GCTEA is doing and planning, and ask their support.*

Additional insight into the objections to the educational television station in Cleveland was provided by GCTEA member and Cleveland Museum of Art Instructor Dr. Gertrude Hornung, who testified in favor of S.B. 205 before Congress in 1960. Back in 1952, the FCC had allotted three UHF stations to the Cleveland broadcast area, one of which was reserved for educational purposes. In her testimony before Congress, Dr. Hornung alluded to opposition on the part of one unnamed VHF station to all UHF broadcasting for two reasons: one, there was rumored to be complete conversion to all UHF stations for all purposes other than military and defense, and second, perhaps more realistically, UHF would cut into VHF audiences. "Whether this is very logical or valid, it exists as an opposition, and that is all I am saying," noted Hornung. When asked whether the objections were openly expressed, Hornung stated, "The opposition has not been an open one; it has been on more of lack of encouragement of this present activity." Added Dr. Hornung, "The main difficulty, I believe has been this great problem of getting the true information over to the public, and also to get this beginning 'seed' money."

GCTEA vs. Cleveland Board of Education: The Gloves Are Off

Still, there was more bickering between the Cleveland School Board and the GCTEA regarding educational television. In early 1961, the board pushed to get a two-year, 0.4 mil levy on the ballot for ETV, while the GCTEA warned against it. Norma Wulff of the Cleveland School Board accused the GCTEA of being "high-handed and aggressive" and complained that "people who don't know anything about our problems shouldn't be fooling around with them." Wulff insisted that the Cleveland School system should build and retain control of the station but felt that other school systems should be asked to contribute to its funding. Walter Davis of the school board felt that "if we are ever to get educational TV in greater Cleveland, the Cleveland Board of Education will have to take the first step." While Davis acknowledged that the GCTEA was made up of "fine people, they are never going to get off the ground."

The GCTEA took a major step forward in contracting the highly qualified Dr. John Schwarzwalder as director of the organization. Schwarzwalder founded the first ETV station in the nation, KUHT, in Houston in 1953. Four years later he initiated KTCA ETV in St. Paul, Minnesota. In Cleveland, Schwarzwalder pleaded for cooperation between all educational and business elements to support the GCTEA.

Congress Acts, and a Truce Is Declared

In 1962, after a five-year campaign, Congress finally enacted the Educational Television Facilities Act, which created a $32 million program of matching federal grants to construct educational television facilities.

Later that year, Congress passed the All-Channel Receiver Act, which required that all TV sets shipped between states feature both VHF and UHF tuners. Both of these acts provided the encouragement that the GCTEA desperately needed.

Wisely, the heads of Cleveland public and parochial schools chose to bury the proverbial hatchets and finally join the concerned citizen members of the GCTEA to form a new organization, the Educational Television Association of Metropolitan Cleveland (ETAMC), in the spring of 1962. Chaired by Cleveland attorney Lewis S. Peirce, the forty-five-member board was composed of former trustees of the GCTEA, including Cleveland Schools Superintendent William Levenson; former superintendent Mark Schinnerer; Monsignor Charles Elwell, Superintendent of Cleveland Catholic Schools; and George Baird of the Cleveland Educational Research Council. As the first order of business, the ETAMC applied to the Cleveland Foundation for a much-needed $30,000 grant. By July, the coveted award was theirs. Meanwhile, John Schwarzwalder returned to the Twin Cities ETV. Consequently, the ETAMC used the funds to hire Dr. Richard Hull, director of Ohio State University's Telecommunications Center (WOSU) and chairman of the Ohio Educational Television Network Commission, as consultant for Cleveland's ETV project.

But Not All Is Quiet

With the grant in hand and the ETAMC taking shape, one might think that the mission to build Cleveland's educational television station would proceed peacefully. Nothing could be further from the truth. While the ETAMC favored a closed-circuit television system, former GCTEA member Richard S. Luntz, vice-president of the Luntz Iron and Steel Company, staunchly argued that a four-channel open-system, proposed by one manufacturer would serve Cleveland, its suburbs and other nearby cities such as Akron, Canton, and Youngstown. Closed-circuit is carried by wire; signals from an open circuit system could be picked up anywhere. Luntz felt that open-circuit system would receive more public support. Louis S. Peirce, head of the ETAMC, felt that "a debate on this now would impede rather than expedite the project." Peirce publicly referred to Luntz as a "a dedicated man but not a team player." One month later, Richard Hull submitted a report to the ETAMC recommending the multi-channel, open-circuit system. Engineering consultant Lew North from the FCC felt that the proposal was within the spirit of FCC policy and should be submitted for FCC approval as soon as possible. The application was finally made in January 1964. The next month, Betty Cope, former producer at WEWS and independent producer of political advertisements, was named to the ETAMC.

More heated discussions followed, this time concerning the broadcast signals. The ETAMC had settled on a transmitter located in North Royalton on property owned by WERE radio. It was believed that signals broadcast from this site would reach Cleveland and the immediately neighboring counties. Consistent with his argument that Channel 25 should serve areas as far away as Youngstown, Luntz, along with L.C. Michelson of Republic Steel, vehemently insisted that the transmitter should be located in Streetsboro, Ohio, near exit 13 of the Ohio Turnpike. Ultimately, for practical reasons, the North Royalton transmitter location won out.

The Check's in the Mail

Looming largely in all of these debates was the all-important question of finances. Louis Peirce announced that the cost to the students of the viewing area would be $1.00 per student per year. Dr. Richard Hull reported that at least $1.25 million in funding was needed for broadcasting equipment. He projected that the sum would originate from foundations, businesses, and the community. But Cleveland rose to the occasion. Amazingly, Storer Broadcasting, owner of rival station WJW TV-8, contributed $20,000 to the ETAMC. There was even support from labor: the Cleveland AFL-CIO chipped in $5,000 toward the station. Major Cleveland businesses, including Republic Steel, pledged a combined total of $200,000. Moreover, local charitable bequest funds were certainly generous. The Leonard C Hanna Jr. Fund donated $75,000, and an equal amount was contributed by the Louis D. Beaumont Fund. Cleveland-area schools pledged $337,000 toward annual operating expenses, which amounted to $1 per student per year.

But the biggest break came in September 1964 when the U.S Department of Health, Education and Welfare (HEW) awarded a grant of $250,000 to the ETAMC for the creation of the educational television station. Of course, it didn't hurt that the secretary of the HEW was none other than Anthony J. Celebrezze, former mayor of the city of Cleveland.

WVIZ, I SEE!

That fall, major announcements were made regarding Cleveland's educational television station. First, Betty Cope was named general manager of the new station. The call letters of the station were to be WVIZ. Chris Henry, Betty's niece recalled years later, "On a Sunday when we were all at the cabin, Betty asked me to bring my Latin textbook, and we spent the afternoon trying out different Latin-based words as call letters, finally coming up with WVIZ." In Latin, the abbreviation *viz* translates "to see." Perhaps Betty was following Pittsburgh's choice of the call letters WQED; the Latin abbreviation *qed* translates to "what was to be shown."

Further, it was announced that Channel 25 would operate out of studios located in the Max S. Hayes Trade School, 4600 Detroit Avenue. The cost of the transmission equipment plus two large cameras totaled $600,000.

The inaugural broadcast was scheduled for February 1, 1965. "We are ready to go," Betty proclaimed confidently. "We are ready and ready to serve." But in keeping with the drama that set the stage for educational television in Cleveland, uncontrollable factors intervened. On Saturday, January 30, the antenna was raised. Connecting work between the antenna and ground wires still needed to be finished. As lake effect fate would have it, a major storm dumped twelve inches of snow on northeast Ohio, and temperatures hovered around zero, so the final connection was delayed. Continued cold weather and high winds prevented the final rigging touches on the transmitter for another six days. At WVIZ's "Great Idea Award" ceremony in 2009, Betty remembered that "Congressman [William E.] Minshall heard of our plight and offered his helicopter to lower the equipment into place. Elated, I headed for the antenna farm and the

Betty Cope was announced as general manager of WVIZ in 1965. *Author's collection.*

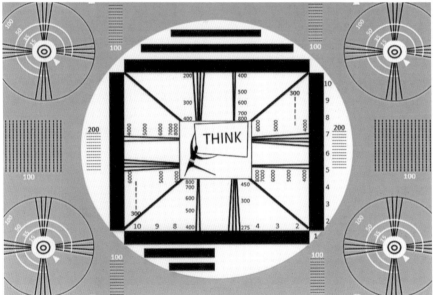

Top: Max Hayes High School in Cleveland was the site of WVIZ's first studios. *Author's collection.*

Bottom: "THINK" test pattern for WVIZ, which was shown on its inaugural broadcast, February 7, 1965. *Ideastream archives.*

National Educational Television (NET) logo from 1962. *Ideastream archives.*

crew chief rolled his eyes at me with that look, 'Bah! Women!' Needless to say, we didn't get on the air that day."

Finally, on Sunday, February 7, 1965, at 10:40 a.m., Cleveland's educational television station, WVIZ, went on the air and broadcast a test pattern featuring the word "THINK." At 3:00 p.m., the station aired its first educational program. The broadcast day ended at 10:00 p.m.. WVIZ was now the one hundredth educational television station in the United States. Betty reportedly exclaimed, "This is a wonderful day!" Louis Peirce issued a statement thanking all the "foundations, corporations, and individuals" who contributed money to start the station. "We pledge to them, the schools who are participating in our program and financially supporting it and to the entire community that we will use this fine new facility to provide enrichment on all levels of education and learning." Betty predicted that the first live program would be produced by March 1965.

At last, Betty's dream of bringing quality television to her beloved Cleveland community became a reality. During her thirteen years in commercial television, she painfully observed how her cherished medium, once brimming with stimulating live dramatic programs and scintillating, witty comedy sketches, degraded into a mere distributor of banal, mindless sitcoms, implausible westerns, and rigged quiz shows. Now was her chance to not only educate children but also restore the thought-provoking entertainment that once dominated the airwaves.

While the daytime hours would bring such programs as *Read Me a Story* and films on geography, mathematics, history, and literature for school instruction, the evening hours, Betty reported, would be filled with cultural programming of drama and music. With the Heart Association of Northeast Ohio, she planned midday programs with lecturers from Cleveland hospitals and universities to help doctors catch up on the latest techniques, surgical and otherwise, to treat heart disease. She envisioned similar training programs for the steel and automotive industries.

Evening programs shown during WVIZ's first week of broadcasting featured recent shows from the National Educational Television (NET) network library in New York, including dramatizations of Shakespeare's *Twelfth Night* and H.H. Munro and Guy de Maupassant short stories; ragtime piano, jazz, and blues performances; Pablo Casals's master cello class; *Adventures in Indonesia*; Mae West singing "Frankie and Johnnie" (as for being on ETV, she quipped, "Honey, all my shows are educational"); and a performance by the San Francisco Symphony. As PD TV critic Alvin Beam put it,

> *Educational television got off to a fine satisfying start last week without any special attempt to put best shows forward....There was no shouting. There was no showcasing....Educational television, though geared to young minds in daytime broadcasts to schools, is not geared that way, especially for its evening and Sunday programming. I find this situation rather pleasant myself and simply recommend to any objectors that may turn up that they look the programs over and then make their own arrangements in their own households.*

What a way to start!

6

The Good Old Max Hayes Days

At the annual ETAMC meeting in October 1965, Betty Cope was named general manager of WVIZ. The station had been on the air for eight months, mainly broadcasting tapes of programs that had been shipped from the NET New York headquarters. The early success of the station could be attributed to Betty's shrewd business sense and her own early television work. Just as she had learned from James Hanrahan at WEWS some eighteen years earlier, the key to any successful management role was to surround oneself with a talented, diligent staff. In her own evolution from receptionist to floor director to program director, she found that television experience was not as crucial as a willingness to learn and a zeal for broadcasting. This was never better exemplified than in the case of Larry Tressler, who is likely the only surviving member of WVIZ's Max Hayes studio crew and a veritable treasure trove of memories. An enormous debt of gratitude is owed to Mr. Tressler for generously sharing his recollections.

To properly present this tale of broadcasting history, this chapter is divided into two segments. The first portion is devoted to the Max Hayes studio and its dedicated and resourceful technical staff, while the second discusses the talented on-air and behind-the-scenes producers of the successful educational and informational programs that were broadcast from that primitive studio.

The Technical Staff: Hitting the Airwaves Without Making Error-waves

Now that they had survived the long and arduous journey to reach the airwaves, the staff at Cleveland's educational television station worked hard to broadcast on a shoestring budget. WVIZ's first facilities at Max Hayes High School were cramped, which made for some daunting technical challenges. While some new equipment was purchased with the Cleveland Foundation and HEW grants, most of the instrumentation was modest at best, mainly consisting of donations from the city's three network stations. As a consequence, cameras of various vintages were used in the studio. What they lacked in space and equipment, the station staff made up in enthusiasm.

In 1966, seventeen-year-old Max Hayes electronics major Larry Tressler was thrilled to learn that the educational station was looking for student workers. After an informal interview, he was hired on the spot to sort and box study guides for schools that were viewing educational programs. "So much for the excitement of broadcasting," sighed Tressler.

At Max Hayes, the gymnasium also served as a theatrical stage. For the new station, the stage would also double as a studio. According to Tressler, "I truly believe they picked Max Hayes School to be the first home of WVIZ because of the useless space in its gym. We used the stage occasionally for

News media identification card for Larry Tressler, station engineer at WVIZ's Max Hayes studios in the 1960s and '70s. *Larry Tressler collection.*

school assemblies, and the yearly senior graduation, but that was it…Without a drama club, or theater department, it was never fully used."

The studio, as Tressler remembered, was "small but cavernous. It measured thirty by twenty by sixty feet. Unfortunately, the sixty feet was straight up. It extended from the floor to the roof of the second floor. It created a lot of echoes and headaches for the audio engineers. We tried hanging lots of drapes, heavy fabrics, and rugs to deaden the sound. It was usable, but never great." The crew soon found that it was necessary for performers to use lavalier microphones, since boom microphones would result in a "cave" effect.

A floor-to-ceiling wall was constructed as a backdrop for the studio. However, no one at the station thought about the gym classes that were being conducted behind the backdrop. "Any noises from the gym could be heard through the wall and would ruin the recordings," said Tressler. "Eventually we made the decision to record shows after school and early evenings."

Following his mailroom assignment, Tressler worked for the station's art department. Taped educational shows from NET were only twenty-eight minutes in length. Without commercials, station technicians were faced with the dilemma of two minutes of "dead air" at the end of each program. "During these breaks, the station would show a 'Coming Up' slide. This was a slide in a film projector of our stick figure mascot pointing to the name of the next program to be shown," said Tressler. "I would create these on a 'Line O Scribe' printing press with real type and printer's ink, photograph them, process the film, and then put them between two small square pieces of glass to make a photographic slide. I also printed all the diplomas we sent to people that completed our TV courses."

Long before the mantra of workplace "teamwork" became popular, WVIZ's early employees wore many hats. The station owed its early success to the dedication of its versatile staff. As Tressler remembered, "Warren Mostek was in charge of the art department, was studio supervisor, jack of all trades, my mentor, and best friend for my entire career, and the rest of his life. You could find him wherever the action was. Whether it be building sets, running camera, or setting up equipment on a cold and wet high school football field. He was the best.

"Our engineering staff did wonders to keep the equipment working. Ralph Campbell supervised the engineering staff and was a real 'hands on' guy. Bill Anderson was an engineer who was super friendly, and got me interested in being an audio engineer. Juan Millian was a really great maintenance engineer. Later I ended up working with Juan again at WUAB TV 43 in Parma.

"Our studio crew was small but mighty. Bill Crite taught me a lot about the studio, and life in general, in the few years he was there. Then there was Nev Chandler. He was part of the crew but then got promoted to being our staff announcer.

"We only had two directors on staff, but they did it all. Mike Kroger and Jay Edsel consistently worked with a zero budget, but constantly produced exceptional programs.

"I was studio crew, building and assembling the sets, lighting director, TV camera operator, and floor director. I was also being trained as audio engineer and emergency fill-in booth announcer. Their small staff of professionals performed miracles, putting together programs with next to no budget. The technical staff made things happen that were electronically impossible. Somehow, we all pulled together to make it happen week, after week, after week.

"I learned so much from all the talented technical staff. I will never be able to thank them enough," recalled Tressler. "They started me on my broadcasting career that would take me through my fifty-plus years in TV and radio. I will always cherish those early years at WVIZ and regret that I didn't take more pictures."

CREATIVE MINDS: BUILDING A TALENTED TEAM TO EDUCATE VIEWERS

WVIZ's educational broadcasting service took off in a flash. In 1965, many school districts began to subscribe to the on-the-air instruction service, including Bedford, Berea, Brecksville, Cleveland, Cleveland Heights–University Heights, Fairview Park, Independence, Lakewood, Mayfield, North Olmsted, Richmond Heights, Rocky River, Shaker Heights, Solon, South Euclid, Strongsville, Warrensville Heights, Willoughby-Eastlake, Painesville, Twinsburg, and Kenston in Geauga County. Some other school districts such as Euclid and Bay Village needed more time for financial planning; in other words, they were waiting for passage of tax levies.

However, one major school district opted for a different televised service for its classrooms. Since 1961, the Parma School District had used an ETV system that originated at Purdue University, named the Midwest Program on Airborne Television Instruction (MPATI). For six hours a day, a DC-6 airplane flew figure eights over Indiana and, through an amazing technique

Betty Cope illustrating "Coming Up" slide cards, which were shown between educational programs, circa 1965. *CSU Memory Project.*

known as "Stratovision," lowered an immense antenna from its belly and broadcast taped educational programs. Through a translator tower located on Parma School Board Property, the plane signals were rebroadcast to subscribing local schools. At least five school districts received instructional programming from both MPATI and WVIZ. Parma, because of the necessity of converting sets to receive Channel 25, stuck with MPATI for seven years. Needless to say, MPATI was an expensive and cumbersome service and was discontinued in 1968 due to lack of subscriber funds. Eventually, Parma schools tuned into WVIZ for classroom instruction.

Alan Stephenson was an alumnus of MPATI, having created numerous programs for the service over its short lifespan. He also initiated educational television shows for Ohio State University's Campus Cable System as well as the State of Massachusetts educational television system.

With his rich background in ETV, Alan Stephenson was the first person Betty Cope hired for Cleveland's newest station. As a test pattern with the word THINK was shown on Sunday, February 7, 1965, at 10:40 a.m., Stephenson made the very first on-air announcement, "This is WVIZ, Cleveland's educational television station." Stephenson was named the first director of WVIZ's educational services department.

In the vulnerable first years of the station, Betty Cope's business acumen helped her recognize that in order to keep her station afloat, she needed to find a way of making money. Without commercials, she had to sell a product: educational programs. Stephenson served as executive producer for dozens of local instructional television productions, always trying to keep the shows within their meager budget. In June 1965, it was announced that WVIZ would present seven original educational series in the fall: two series would be dedicated to art, two to music, two to science, and one to social studies. Where more than one was planned per subject, separate series would be aimed at different age levels. Seven teachers were selected from a group of forty who auditioned to instruct on the air. Brenda Veal and Elaine Shakely were recruited to teach music, Bob Crumpler and Judy Magalegna were chosen as science instructors, Mary Jo Mehl was selected as a social studies teacher, and Carol Bosley and Margaret Higginbotham were hired to teach art.

Having been steeped in culture from an early age, Betty favored an enrichment approach to television instruction rather than traditional classroom edification. For instance, some classes featured groups from music departments of local colleges that demonstrated various instruments. For social studies programs, community development topics were explored by filming and interviewing leaders in northeast Ohio.

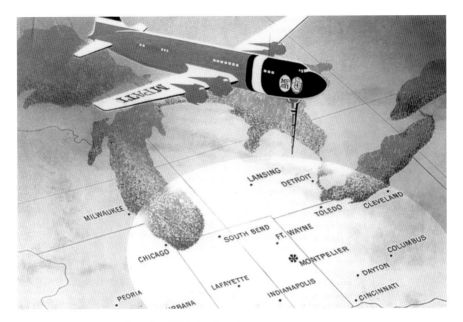

A 24-foot mast houses a single, two-channel, high-gain antenna. It is hydraulically operated and gyroscopically stabilized so it remains vertical. The antenna gives an effective radiated power of 50 kilowatts visual and five kilowatts aural.

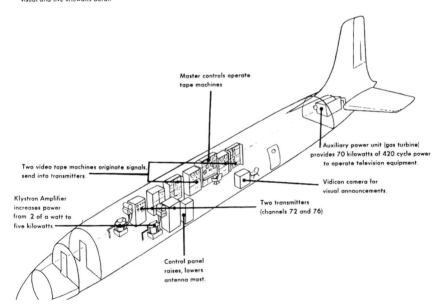

Top: Illustration of MPATI Stratovision broadcast program, 1950s. *Ohio State University*.

Bottom: Schematic illustration of MPATI Stratovision airplane, 1950s. *From* Radio-Television News *January 1950.*

Alan Stephenson was the first director of Educational Services for WVIZ, pictured here circa 1966. *NE OH TV Memories.*

Under Betty's guidance, Stephenson quickly nurtured the local talent. A gifted music graduate of Baldwin-Wallace who also performed as a soprano with Karamu House, the charming Brenda Veal created her own music instruction program titled *Stepping into Rhythm*. The show, which was aimed at first and second graders, was marketed nationwide and quickly became a hit.

Bob Crumpler, a WEWS reporter, presented a total of nine different science-oriented programs on WVIZ, including *Search for Science*. Crumpler not only performed on-the-air experiments à la Mr. Wizard but also profiled various trades such as masonry. As Larry Tressler remembered, "They were always a blast to be a part of. You never knew if his experiments were going to work or not. I'd seen him getting burned, suffer electrical shocks and bitten by animals. But he always made it look good."

One of Bob Crumpler's shows focused on zoology and featured animals from the Cleveland Metroparks Zoo, which resulted in some rather unpredictable situations on live television. "I was the 'off camera' person who handed animals to him on his show." Tressler recalled. "I handed him practically anything you can imagine. One week, a monkey was a featured animal. I had the monkey nearby on a leash, but he was acting up. I decided that if I let him explore around a bit while still on leash, he might calm down. He then climbed a studio curtain about ten feet into the air. That's when Bob called for the monkey. I started pulling gently on the leash while whispering, 'Come down monkey.' Bob called again getting no response from me or the monkey. When he asked for the third time, I pulled hard on the leash and said 'GET DOWN!' The monkey fell

Right: Carol Bosley instructed art classes on WVIZ from the 1960s through the 1980s. *Carter Edman collection.*

Below: Bob Crumpler presented science education programs at WVIZ and was a newscaster for WEWS. *NE OH TV Memories.*

with a thud, hitting his head on the floor. He was completely knocked out. Knowing that the show must go on, I picked up the monkey's limp lifeless body and handed him to Bob. Bob then went on to explain to the kids that the monkey is sleeping soundly and must be really tired. After another minute, Mr. Monkey woke up and was very cooperative for the rest of the show. I was glad he was alive and I still had a job. But the monkey and I never became friends."

Crumpler's shows were also well-received and were sold to many other stations. Given the atmosphere of racial turbulence of the 1960s, the wide appeal of the two hosts was rather unique, as both Veal and Crumpler were African American. Betty's promotion of Veal's and Crumpler's programs demonstrated that her dedication to quality broadcasting lay far beyond the social norms of the time. Rather than bowing to convention, she chose television educators based on their abilities. By 1967, nearly 300,000 students in northeast Ohio were receiving televised instruction from WVIZ. The successful sales of these classroom programs proved to be a significant source of funding for WVIZ in its formative years.

Bringing Home High School Sports

Yet there was still another way that WVIZ would connect with northeast Ohio schools. Local high school sports were enormously popular, but none of the network affiliates broadcast any of the games. Betty Cope and her staff decided to dedicate Friday nights to local high school football, basketball, and wrestling. After the outdated donated cameras were replaced with newer RCA models, station technicians fitted a remote truck with the old cameras. This they took to many high school football fields and gymnasiums to provide game coverage. Larry Tressler reminisced, "I was the field camera operator for the first few years of 'on location' high school sports on Friday nights. Mike Massa broadcast the play-by-play. We as a crew froze our asses off every Friday night bringing those football games to you. We would record the games live-to-tape. We'd record the first half of a football game and have a runner rush the recorded video tape back to the station to hit the 10:00 p.m. airtime. The crew would record the second half, strike all the equipment and get back to the station in time to see the remainder of the game we were just at. It was pretty exciting."

Mike Massa was WVIZ's first sports director and announced local high school football and basketball games. *Gary Bluhm collection.*

Northeast Ohio's weather frequently presented a challenge for broadcasting Friday night high school football in northeast Ohio. WVIZ field services engineer Dick Barnick remembered a particularly treacherous night at Orange High School field. "The camera operators would always sit on top of a scaffold. One night, the wind actually blew over the scaffold! Fortunately no one was hurt, but it was pretty wild." Despite hazardous weather conditions, Friday night football, and especially its announcer, were remembered fondly by the engineering staff. Said videographer Gary Manke, "Mike was always enthusiastic about everything, and he would often misspeak. Once, instead of the 'line of scrimmage,' he burst out the 'line of spinach.' He was a real hoot."

Educational Television Is for Adults, Too!

Betty saw to it that WVIZ's role as a source of instruction was not just limited to the schools but extended to industry as well. In 1966, the station formed the "WVIZ Television Training Institute" to offer televised in-plant training series. More than one hundred companies enrolled employees in series concerning management and supervisory methods and communication. One program, *Supervising the Disadvantaged*, was created in partnership with Cleveland State University. Plant managers were instructed about urban economics and ways to develop employees' skills.

Moreover, Betty found a way to attract evening television viewers. She drew on Cleveland's rich cultural community to create intriguing programs for adults. The witty and always opinionated *Cleveland Press* columnist and novelist Don Robertson was given his own program on WVIZ, *Robertson at Large*. Robertson, a Cleveland native, gained a following as a no-nonsense, tell-it-like-it-is television talk show host. On his set, which was assembled from thrift store furniture, the curmudgeonly Robertson did not stick to time cues and just continued the show until he had nothing left to say. Station management moved his show to the final time slot of the day so that he could keep talking as long as he wanted. By the mid-1960s, his historic novels had become quite popular, and critics compared his writing style to Mark Twain and Booth Tarkington. Robertson's renown as an author plus the success of his local show enabled Betty to sell his program to numerous educational TV stations across the country.

Colorful author and *Cleveland Press* columnist Don Robertson hosted an early talk show on WVIZ in the late 1960s. *CSU Memory Project.*

The colorful Eugenia Thornton was another of Betty's recruits for nighttime programming. Known in Cleveland as the bibliophile's bibliophile, Thornton was for many years the *Plain Dealer* book reviewer and champion of local literature and drama. In the mid-1960s, Eugenia hosted her eponymous television show with the same warmth and intimacy as she would a book discussion group, sharing her passion for novels and biographies and inspiring viewers to head for their local libraries to check out her latest recommendations. The enthusiasm and charm that she exuded on her Tuesday evening

Betty Cope receives a check for $100,000 from Art Watson (*left*), vice-president of WKYC, Cleveland's NBC affiliate. Louis Peirce, chairman of the Educational Television Association of Metropolitan Cleveland (ETAMC), is shown at right, 1965. *CSU Memory Project.*

programs were contagious; with her melodious voice, she somehow fostered a greater appreciation of the printed word among those who were glued to their television sets. Betty had no trouble marketing Eugenia's show to other cities' educational television stations.

Additional funds started rolling into the new station. NBC, which had recently acquired ownership of its local affiliate WKYC (formerly KYW), donated $100,000 to WVIZ for equipment and instructional programming. In 1966, the Department of Health, Education and Welfare awarded a grant of $75,000 to WVIZ, which was then matched by $75,000 from area donors. Locally, the Martha Holden Jennings Association donated $50,000 for the production of new programs in music and the humanities.

In its first two years of existence, WVIZ's locally produced offerings complemented the educational, public affairs, music specials, and dramatic programs that were shown through NET. By the spring of 1967, the *Plain Dealer* editors proclaimed "WVIZ—Rate it Excellent!" and sang the praises of the home-grown programs. Yet it was becoming clear that with an increasing program base and expanding staff, the station was outgrowing the Max Hayes studios. Larger quarters would soon become available, but like everything else for WVIZ, nothing was easy; time, toil, and tenacity were needed to make the new headquarters a reality.

7

From Earth-Moving
to Mind-Moving

The period between 1965 and 1980 was one of tremendous growth for WVIZ—physically, financially, and perhaps most importantly, creatively. It was not without its growing pains, but it was certainly an interesting metamorphosis.

WE'RE MOVING ON UP TO BROOKPARK ROAD

In late January 1967, the ETAMC announced that it had purchased the Marks Tractor building located at 4300 Brookpark Road for the new WVIZ studios. Transforming a tractor supply warehouse into a television studio was no easy feat. Former WVIZ studio technician Larry Tressler remembers the day in the spring of 1967 when he first visited the recently purchased edifice. "I expected to see a building that once housed tractors like Massey Ferguson, John Deere or maybe even a Toro, or Cub Cadet. No way! This was a company that worked on HEAVY excavation equipment. Bull dozers and steam shovels. The stuff you see moving large amounts of earth." Years of twenty-ton vehicles traversing the warehouse had taken their toll on the building's interior space, leaving the floors as a heap of broken concrete rubble and walls that were covered with cement dust. "The interior resembled a bombed-out building in a World War II movie," said Tressler. Following an extensive cleanup operation, a fresh layer of concrete was poured to create new floors, and new concrete walls were built. Electricians completely rewired the building. The enormous service bay of the warehouse eventually became the new Studio A.

Soon it was time to move into the newly remodeled studio. As compared to the old Max Hayes studios, which housed about twenty light fixtures, the size of the new studio required about two hundred. When the brand-new, pricey Colortran lights were delivered, Tressler recalled, "We spent a good week unboxing, assembling, and hanging them. It was like Christmas morning." For the technicians who struggled through the primitive high school studio surroundings, it was undoubtedly an exciting time to be part of a new broadcasting facility.

The Brookpark Road studio was located only about five miles from Max Hayes Trade School, so the technicians carefully packed and moved the existing equipment into a rented truck and transported it themselves. In one of the last truckloads, a few of the set pieces and the studio camera pedestals or wheelbases of the cameras were transported. While the camera pedestals have large horizontal steering wheels that enable the operators to change directions, they have no brakes. To keep the pedestals from moving

Marks Tractor showroom and warehouse at 4300 Brookpark Road, which WVIZ purchased for its new studios, circa 1963. *Author's collection.*

Betty Cope with blueprints for new WVIZ studios on Brookpark Road, circa 1966. *CSU Memory Project.*

around the truck, the technicians placed 2x4s around the pedestal bases and nailed the boards to the truck floor. "We decided it good idea for us to ride in the back with the equipment just to keep an eye on it all," Tressler remembered. "If the truck was driven slowly, what could possibly go wrong?"

Not long after the trip started, the pedestals, which each weighed about three hundred pounds, broke loose from their supports and started rolling around the truck. Jumping up, the technicians tried their best to stop the rolling monstrosities. Noted Larry Tressler, "As we rode them like mechanical bulls, we tried to control their direction with the steering wheels. Fat chance! We helplessly crashed into the set pieces, breaking most of them, and into all four walls of the trailer. We also banged into each other resembling a demolition derby at the county fair."

The brand-new concrete walls of the studio looked great, but they created headaches for the sound engineers. To lessen the echo effect, it was necessary for the technicians to climb atop scaffolding platforms and glue rigid acoustical tiles to the ceilings. "The glue that was recommended was a tar-like substance with the smell of rotten stinky walnuts," said Tressler. "We would put four golf ball-size scoops of this smelly mess on each panel, then held the panel to the ceiling for a couple of minutes for it to adhere. We referred to this job as 'making the walnuts.'" To Tressler, the job seemed endless. "I ruined many sets of clothes with that sticky smelly walnut goo. But somehow we made it fun."

Finally, the station commenced its operation from the new studios on September 6, 1967. Outside the new station, other improvements were made. A 200-foot tower was raised on the top of the new Brookpark Road studio for limited transmission at a 2500 MHz band to local schools with special receiving equipment. The broadcast range was approximately twenty miles. According to Louis Peirce, the tower would increase the station's capacity to broadcast programs without raising cost of one dollar per student per year for participating schools. About five miles south of the station in North Royalton, a new 812-foot-tall tower was built. This transmitter, it was reported, would allow WVIZ to double its signal power.

By the time of its third birthday in 1968, WVIZ, which used to serve nineteen school systems and a few thousand homes, now served forty-four school districts and 600,000 homes with a rich mixture of drama, issues, sports, and thought. WVIZ made great strides in its first three years of existence. But for Betty to sustain her dream of educational broadcasting to her beloved northeast Ohio community, much financing

Moving day at the Brookpark Road studios of WVIZ, August 2, 1967. *Ideastream archives.*

A Cleveland-area billboard advertises the new educational TV station in the 1960s. *Ideastream archives.*

would be needed. She had heard of San Francisco's success with televised auctions—why not do the same in Cleveland? In May 1968, WVIZ's first televised auction was held, and a Cleveland television institution was born. The annual auction was such an important part of WVIZ history that a separate chapter is devoted to it (see chapter 8, "Hey, Kids, Let's Put on a Show!")

As the station's popularity grew, several organizations expressed interest in presenting educational broadcasts through its facilities. The Cleveland Board of Education and the Diocese of Cleveland, which operates Cleveland Catholic Schools, joined with WVIZ in petitioning the FCC for twelve new instructional channels. Ultimately, the FCC approved the assignment of sixteen new ultra-high frequency channels to the northeast Ohio area. The sixteen channels were selected by a board that consisted of members of the ETAMC, the Cleveland Commission on Higher Education, the Cleveland Board of Education, the Cleveland Catholic Diocese, the Cuyahoga County Superintendents Association, the Educational Research Council, the Parma Board of Education, and the Cleveland Medical Association.

PBS IS BORN

Concurrent with the growth of WVIZ was the evolution of the concept of public broadcasting. Major changes were coming at the network level of educational television. A brief history of the educational television network begins with the National Educational Television and Radio Center (NETRC), which first formed in 1958 and aired local educational shows and imported BBC dramas for nighttime broadcasting. In November 1963, NETRC divested its radio assets and changed its name to National Educational Television (NET). By the mid-1960s, NET had begun to broadcast controversial documentaries on social issues such as racism and poverty. Some of these shows, such as *NET Journal*, were critically acclaimed but drew complaints from conservative markets.

In 1966, President Lyndon Johnson called on the Carnegie Foundation to conduct an investigation on the future of educational television. The Carnegie Commission Report of 1967 recommended that educational television be transformed into "public television" by a separate organization.

Logo for the new Public Broadcasting Service (PBS) in 1970. *Ideastream archives.*

In 1967, Congress passed the Public Broadcasting Act, which established the Corporation for Public Broadcasting (CPB). The CPB was a private nonprofit corporation funded by taxpayers to disburse grants to public broadcasters. It was managed by a nine-member board appointed by the president and approved by the Senate. The main role of the CPB was to funnel government support to public TV stations and producers throughout the United States. Further, the CPB was charged with the task of helping local stations to create innovative programs and increase public broadcasting throughout the country.

The Public Broadcasting Service (PBS) was founded in November 1969. NET continued to produce socially minded programs and became the target of criticisms of government partisanship. The Ford Foundation and the CPB shut down the operations of NET and replaced it with PBS, which would serve only as a distributor of public television programming. Unlike NET, PBS would not be directly involved with any television production. External producers and local stations would provide the programming for PBS. For example, in the fall of 1969, the Children's Television Workshop produced *Sesame Street* and sold it to PBS; with the universal appeal of the Muppets and catchy songs, the show immediately became a major hit for PBS, winning viewers among children and adults alike. The template of PBS serving as a supplier of externally produced programs remains to this day.

Ford Funding Drives Away...

While the CPB was created to help channel federal funding, a blow to foundational educational television funding came in the form of a federal tax reform bill that passed in 1969. The bill imposed a 100 percent tax penalty on foundations and a 50 percent penalty on foundation managers if they made grants that might have an effect on legislation or influence elections. This meant that any public affairs or news-related program could not be financed by a foundation. In addition, the bill provided for the imposition of a 7.5 percent tax on the investment income of private foundations, which would come out of grants to public broadcasting. In the past, the Ford Foundation awarded general grant monies to educational television stations for unspecified purposes. But the situation changed drastically under the new tax bill. As columnist Jack Gould lamented in the *New York*

Times, public broadcasting "has become entangled in the determination of some members of Congress to curb the activist role of the Ford Foundation in a wide variety of educational, cultural, and social affairs." Under the leadership of McGeorge Bundy, president, and Fred W. Friendly, former head of CBS and television consultant, the Ford Foundation decided to make specific grants to specific programs that met with their approval. If the Ford Foundation did not directly approve WVIZ's programming, it would mean the loss of $185,000.

…BUT THE COMMUNITY PULLS TOGETHER

Winning Ford's approval for program financing seemed to be more trouble than it was worth. Other stations were making it on their own with public funding; WVIZ would simply have to perform the same feat with funding from the annual Auction and pledges from viewers. Sidney H. Smith, retired manager of GM Parma Transmission Plant, was chosen by WVIZ's board of directors to lead the 1969 Capital Funds Campaign for WVIZ. The goal of the campaign was to raise $600,000 to modernize the station, including $140,000 to convert to color broadcasting, $225,000 to add the sixteen new channels for use in schools, plus $135,000 to construct a third studio and a master control for extra channels. Auctions were now planned as annual fundraising events. Every three months, pledge drives were held in which special programs were broadcast with breaks in which Betty and other staff members requested that viewers call with donations and become station members.

Public funding from northeast Ohio's residents enabled Betty and her staff to freely create informational and locally relevant programming without the foundational approval. The station held mayoral debates and public town hall meetings. The most popular town hall was devoted to proposed changes to the Cleveland Transit System public transportation routes. Volunteers staffed ten phone lines for the town hall; calls to the station came at the rate of two per minute per phone line, mainly from viewers protesting the cost-cutting elimination of various bus lines.

Through the remainder of the 1960s, NBC and WKYC-Channel 3 continued their strong support of WVIZ. The network and its affiliate donated over two hundred pieces of equipment valued at $25,000 to WVIZ in 1967. A complete (used) mobile unit and $110,000 in cash were provided

Top: Betty leads a WVIZ membership pledge drive in the early 1970s. *From the* Akron Beacon Journal *archives*.

Bottom: A Brookpark Road billboard advertises the first WVIZ Auction in 1968. *Ideastream archives*.

by WKYC two years later. The mobile unit was instrumental in advancing WVIZ's coverage of local high school football and basketball games.

THE TODDLER GROWS UP

In February 1970, WVIZ celebrated its fifth anniversary as Betty proclaimed, "And now, we are, as they say on Sesame Street, one, two, three, four, five, five, five, five, five!" At the party, Betty said that she felt "somewhat maternal" toward the station, having been with it since it was "the infant 25." The success of the pledge drives that year filled the void left by the loss of the Ford Foundation grant and enabled WVIZ to begin broadcasting on Saturdays from 5:00 to 11:00 p.m. The growing number of locally produced shows and increased hours of network programs made it difficult to re-broadcast them during the week, so Saturdays were mainly reserved for re-broadcasting.

As PBS network commenced operations, the 1970 fall television lineup was more diverse than ever. "A kaleidoscope," as Betty described it to PD TV columnist Raymond Hart. "We'll have programs on music, drama, ecology, public affairs....You name it, and we'll have it." Indeed, the caliber of evening programs seemed to surpass that of previous years. Sir Kenneth Clark's *Civilisation* chronicled the development of modern society. Consumer affairs were discussed in *The Nader Report*; *San Francisco Mix* documented the lives of young people on the West Coast; *Flick Out* presented the work of young filmmakers; William F. Buckley's Firing Line interviewed various notable guests; and *Black Frontier* illustrated the lives of minorities as they settled across the Great Plains in the nineteenth century. Locally, there were numerous daytime instructional shows, Mike Massa's weekly *Varsity Club*, and Friday night high school sports broadcasts.

By October 1970, WVIZ's creation of dozens of educational programs prompted PBS to rank it in the top 10 of 199 public television stations across the country. At a station trustees' meeting, Martin Essex, state superintendent of public instruction, lauded WVIZ's production of the series *The History of Black Americans* as the first complete study of Black history performed by any network.

More kudos for Betty's work came in the form of the 1970 award for Woman of the Year from the Inter-Club, a council comprising fifteen groups of career women. Reporting on the award, Esther Brightman, club editor

Kenneth Clark was the host of the culturally significant *Civilisation* series on PBS. *Ideastream archives.*

for the *Plain Dealer*, remarked, "To describe Betty is to write the history of WVIZ. She was there as one of the board of trustees when the station was only the dream of a few devoted and persistent persons who foresaw the benefits of non-commercial TV. She was there in 1965 when the station went on the air with her as a general manager. Constantly gathering more and more appreciation and support, she continues to be at the center of the station's advances." Betty was named to the Greater Cleveland Growth Association in 1972 and to the Board of Directors of Blue Cross in 1974. Moreover, in 1975, Ohio governor James Rhodes named Betty as a trustee of Cleveland State University, a position that she held until 1985.

POLITICS MAKES STRANGE FUNDING-FELLOWS

Betty soon found that the turbulent political climate of the early 1970s would shape the future of federal funding for public broadcasting. The Nixon administration's distrust of mass media clouded the outlook for any congressional appropriations for PBS. In a private memo to the president, Clay Whitehead, director of the White House Office of Telecommunications Policy (OTP), stated, "No matter how firm our control of CPB management, public television will always attract liberal and left-wing producers, writers, and commentators. We cannot get Congress to reduce funds for public television or exclude CPB from public affairs programming. But we can reform the structure of public broadcasting to eliminate its worst features." Playing on a perceived

Betty Cope, trustee of Cleveland State University, reviews construction plans for new university gymnasium circa 1975. *CSU Memory Project.*

resentment on the part of local stations toward PBS, Whitehead warned the affiliates that they were just becoming pawns of a centralized network. Whitehead proposed making drastic cuts in CPB funding and directly allocating funds to local stations. According to Whitehead, the key to achieving these goals was to provide the stations with more federal funding than they received from CPB.

In response to Whitehead's proposals, the NAEB's Public Television Managers' Council issued a statement to the effect that while they agreed with the concept of local station orientation, they rejected the notion of circumventing the CPB. While they agreed in principle that federal funding was desperately needed and that CPB should direct that funding, philosophical differences between PBS and CPB had developed. Some PBS board members felt that CPB exercised too much control over programming.

Amid the chaos within the young broadcast organization, the harshest blow to federal funding was dealt. On June 30, 1972, President Nixon vetoed the CPB Authorization Bill, citing the need for increased localization within PBS. According to Nixon, the CPB had become "the center of power and the focal point of control for the entire public broadcasting system."

As a consequence, top CPB officials resigned. Both PBS and the CPB restructured under new management. In 1973, they adopted a partnership agreement that encouraged long-term financing, which would remove public broadcasting from the "annual hazards of political authorization and appropriation" and strengthen local stations' autonomy and independence.

Betty vocalized her concerns on the lack of long-term federal funding dilemma. "The year-to-year basis is a threat to public broadcasting," she stated. "It guarantees one thing—status quo....Growth plans are stunted under such a short-term procedure." Regarding localization, she pointed out that "if, by supporting local stations, you jeopardize the quality of Public Broadcasting Service programming, you are also jeopardizing a source of local income."

Curiously, during his last days in the White House in the summer of 1974, President Nixon submitted a proposal to Congress to provide long-term insulated financing of public broadcasting through a five-year authorization plan. President Ford took up the proposal again in 1975, and by the end of that year, the bill had been signed into law. As a result of this law, the Public Broadcasting Fund was established by the U.S. Treasury. Furthermore, appropriations were allocated for the period from 1975 through 1980. Some funding would be sent directly to local stations, and most importantly, CPB was mandated to consult with PBS. In 1978, the Public Telecommunications Financing Act awarded $2 million to all PBS stations; WVIZ's share was a paltry $100,000. Clearly, Betty and her station had to do their best to face the challenge to acquire the necessary funding through the Auction and local pledge drives.

Instructional Television Is the Staple

During this era, WVIZ's instructional programming production output was staggering. In 1974, a total of thirty-two WVIZ-produced instructional programs were broadcast across the country at the same time. Some of the more memorable programs included *Let's Build a City*, in which Cleveland educator Ruth Kotila led viewers from the history of Indian villages to the complexities of a modern city, including housing, industries, food distribution, and governments. In *Other Families, Other Friends*, Kotila shared views of people and their heritages in homes in Africa, South America, and Asia. WVIZ's cameras transported grade schoolers through fieldtrips in skyscrapers, riverboats, and steelmaking furnaces in *Explorers Unlimited*. Mike Massa visited job sites throughout Cleveland and interviewed professionals and workers of different trades in *Career Opportunities*.

Arts-a-Bound was a unique look at creations originating from various media. Producer-director Gary Valente recalled flying out to San Francisco to film an episode of this educational show about the formation of bubbles of all shapes and sizes in the Bay Area science museum.

Berea schoolteacher Ann McGregor offered warm and interesting reflections on children's books through *Picture Book Park*. McGregor also introduced youngsters to American history through *Stories of America*, which featured vignettes on prominent figures from Christopher Columbus to Theodore Roosevelt.

WVIZ also produced *Inside/Out*, an anthology series of fifteen-minute shorts that were created to instruct children about social issues. *Inside/Out* differed from other shows in that it typically had cliffhanger endings, leaving the children to think about what they might do in similar situations. The locally produced shows became hits and were picked up by numerous stations on a nationwide basis.

Tuning in to the Political Climate of the 1970s

Undoubtedly, the greatest political news stories of the early 1970s centered on President Nixon and the Watergate scandal. Always focusing on the need to inform and educate the public, Betty made the decision in the summer of 1973 to air the Watergate hearings, gavel-to-gavel, during the primetime hours. Interestingly enough, viewer mail to WVIZ proved that the hearings were a hit. By October, however, more calls came to the station requesting a return to regularly scheduled local and PBS cultural programming. A decision was made to air only newsworthy or politically significant portions of the hearings for the remainder of the year.

Cleveland-area journalists provided political insights on WVIZ. *The Danaceau Report* was a weekly program presented by Cleveland radio host and writer Hugh Danaceau and featured interviews with local political leaders and other newsmakers, often discussing issues that

Left: *Cleveland Press* editor Herb Kamm hosted the *Kamm's Corner* talk show on WVIZ. *CSU Memory Project*.

Right: Hugh Danaceau was the host of *The Danaceau Report*, which aired on WVIZ for over twenty years. *CSU Memory Project*.

were relevant to northeast Ohio. Herb Kamm, editor of the *Cleveland Press* and two New York newspapers, hosted his own prime-time talk show titled *Kamm's Corner*. With his contacts on the East Coast and Midwest, Kamm brought a steady stream of celebrities from the political and entertainment worlds to the WVIZ studios for over a decade.

In October 1974, WVIZ presented *An Old-Fashioned Political Rally*, a live, three-hour remote broadcast from the mall in downtown Cleveland. This program gave the public a chance to see and hear candidates for the upcoming November Senate and gubernatorial elections.

Cleveland's leading suffragette, Josephine Irwin (shown here in 1914), was the subject of a WVIZ documentary. *Author's collection.*

Mayoral politics were often profiled on WVIZ. The first African American mayor of a major American city, Cleveland's Carl Stokes, was regularly interviewed in a *Dialog* series on WVIZ in the late 1960s. Later, Mayor Ralph Perk answered questions from viewers about city services in his 1976 program *Direct Line: City Hall*. In the fall of 1979, WVIZ televised mayoral debates between controversial incumbent Dennis Kucinich and challenger George Voinovich, which drew large audiences.

Also in 1979, the drama of local politics took center stage. WVIZ broadcast the *Carnival Kickback Hearings* in which Cleveland City Council president George Forbes was investigated. Allegedly, city hall had protected a carnival kickback gambling scheme. Forbes was ultimately cleared of any charges, but it made for intriguing fodder for viewers who had never before witnessed criminal court proceedings.

Amid the campaign for ratification of the Equal Rights Amendment (ERA) in 1978, WVIZ remembered Cleveland's women's history. *Josephine Irwin, a Civilizing Influence* presented a biography of Cleveland's leading suffragist, who was then eighty-nine years old.

FIGHTING COMMERCIALISM ON PUBLIC TELEVISION

Ohio State University (OSU) announced in 1976 that it would broadcast tapes of its football games on public television stations throughout the state. The only catch was that the broadcasts would include commercial spots promoting the university. Betty took a stand against the concept of commercialism in public television broadcasts and refused to air the games. "Noncommercial television has been free of the constant interruptions of commercial television. Granted, the proposed spot announcements are for a good cause, and it is highly doubtful that viewers would object…but once started down this road, where does it end?" said Betty. "If Ohio State would offer coverage without promotional spots of any kind, we would welcome the opportunity to air the games."

Some incensed viewers complained to the Cleveland newspapers that WVIZ, which for years had aired high school football games, was now demonstrating a lack of support for OSU sports; others praised Betty for her tenacity against commercialism. After much discussion with the OSU staff, a compromise was reached. OSU allowed the state's public television stations the right to edit the promotional spots from the tapes, and WVIZ eventually broadcast six of the season's games.

SHOWCASING THE TALENT

It's often said that a manager is only as good as his or her team. As the station emerged, Betty, like all good managers, surrounded herself with talent. In 1968, she hired a young producer-director from Milwaukee named Frank Strnad. "She called me out of the blue and asked if I would come and interview for the job of production manager," Strnad remembered. "In 1968, no other woman was a general manager of a TV station. She was a strong woman, a great businessperson, and a tough taskmaster. She expected you to do your job. But she never micromanaged." Regarding programming, Strnad recalled, "Betty was very good at designing programs and choosing topics for shows that would be produced locally. She felt that we should create programs that are suited for Cleveland. She was definitely a 'we can do this' sort of person." From 1968 to 1977, Strnad's team produced regular broadcasts of Cleveland City Council meetings. Beginning in 1970, WVIZ aired the Friday Forums of the Cleveland City Club, a nonpartisan debating association, a practice that continues to this day.

Nor did Betty back down from the social issues of the day. *In Both Hands* was an original three-act play dealing with African Americans' search for identity. Written and produced by Cleveland native Annetta Jefferson, the 1970 WVIZ production was the final offering in the Ford Foundation–sponsored *Brother Man* series. *My Soul Looks Back in Wonder*, also produced by Jefferson, told the history of African Americans through music, poetry, and prose. *African Odyssey* documented the story of how Alexander Hamilton Junior High School students realized their dream of traveling to Africa. From fundraising car washes to their first plane trips to embracing the continent's culture, the show was a moving look at the motivation of inner-city students. Another show aimed at the growing youth audience was *Teenage Press Conference*. This monthly *Meet the Press*–type program gave teenagers the opportunity to ask thought-provoking questions of other members of their own age group.

In 1972, PBS announced that it would present a special on venereal disease (VD) hosted by Dick Cavett. Betty decided that WVIZ would take the program one step further. Following the PBS show, WVIZ provided a VD Telethon, in which medical professionals would provide confidential answers to callers' questions off the air. As *Plain Dealer* TV writer Raymond P. Hart put it, "If just one person discovers he or she has venereal disease and receives proper medical aid, it [the program] will be worth it."

Frank Strnad encouraged his team to explore a wide variety of socially relevant topics in unique ways and then present them in a monthly series titled *Director's Showcase*. One memorable episode from 1972, *Fat, Fat, the Water Rat*, took a look at the growing trend toward obesity in the United States and the increasing popularity of weight loss clubs such as Weight Watchers. Another installment presented a day in the life of a long-distance commercial trucker with the camera focused solely on the road. *High on Jesus* brought public attention to Christians living in Geneva, Ohio, who were "turned on to Jesus."

Say Older, My Son, Not Old, was a one-hour local show that probed many aspects of aging, including the physiological, social, and psychological. For 1974, such insights proved to be relatively novel. With a script penned by local resident Everett Dodrill, Betty intended *Say Older* as a pilot for a PBS series envisioned as *The Ageless Life*. Unfortunately, funding from the CPB never materialized, so the series did not come to fruition. A few years later, seniors' habits were once again explored in the local production *Good Old-Fashioned Fitness*. Senior exercise instructor Pat Fromm illustrated ways for the elderly to burn off calories and improve muscle tone.

Spotlight on Cleveland Arts

Some of the most impressive WVIZ productions of this era shone a spotlight on the local arts. On February 25, 1972, WVIZ made television history by airing the first live concert that was simulcast on the radio. As Glass Harp, a rock band whose members included Cleveland and Youngstown musicians, performed live before an audience in the WVIZ studio on Brookpark Road, the performance was broadcast live on WMMS radio. This program actually started a trend for simulcasting national PBS musical performances with local radio stations, including the Metropolitan Opera's *La Bohème* and the Boston Symphony concerts.

WVIZ's showcase of the northeast Ohio arts scene continued throughout the decade. Winning entries of the First Annual Young Filmmaker's Festival were shown on WVIZ in January 1971, with stop-motion animation films of teenagers taking top prizes. In 1973, WVIZ celebrated the fiftieth anniversary of the Cleveland Institute of Music with a special orchestral broadcast. Later that same year, *From High A-Top* presented big-band hits from the Lakeland Jazz Forum. An evening of original dance, *Keritisia*, was directed by choreographer Alex Martin and featured performers from the Ballet Guild of Cleveland. The Dean of the Cleveland Music School Settlement, Clive Lythgoe, performed his own piano compositions in *A Touch of Lythgoe* in 1977.

Local theatrical productions were also highlighted on WVIZ, albeit with great effort. As Strnad remembered, "*Playboy of the Western World* was being performed at Playhouse Square. Betty wanted to bring the entire production to the studio, sets and all. We managed to pull it off. I told Betty she should have had stock in Mayflower Moving. Such unique fare was unheard of in local television."

The rich cultural collections of Cleveland were highlighted in a monthly series titled *Galleries*. Beginning in the fall of 1974, the former director of the Cleveland Museum of Art, Jay Gates, toured Cleveland art galleries and presented everything from ancient Chinese landscapes to modern architecture.

In honor of the bicentennial, *The European Vision of America* took the viewer on a tour of a special exhibition at Cleveland Museum of Art. Host Peter Ustinov presented over one hundred paintings, art objects, and books that depicted early America from the eyes of European artists. Spanning four hundred years, the show illustrated early Europeans' highly imaginative concepts of America's inhabitants. Following a local premiere, the program was broadcast nationally on **PBS**. *Truly American* was another WVIZ program begun during the bicentennial year. This instructional series profiled the lives of prominent figures in early U.S. history and was produced by local Jewish Community Theater director Dorothy Silver.

Creativity in regional programming showcasing the arts continued throughout the 1970s. A local mime troupe's impression of the Christmas season in downtown Cleveland was presented in the silent 1977 WVIZ special *Mime Dreaming of a White Christmas*. A children's tale, *The Little Sweep*, performed by the New Cleveland Opera Company and the Cleveland Orchestra's Children's Chorus, was taped in the WVIZ studios and aired in early 1978. This story of a chimney sweep featured talent from the Cleveland

WVIZ presented *Glass Harp in Concert* live in the studio in 1972. The concert was simulcast on WMMS radio. *Ideastream archives.*

Institute of Music and Baldwin Wallace College. In 1979, WVIZ celebrated the sixtieth anniversary of the Cleveland Orchestra with a special concert telecast that was later shown to a nationwide audience on PBS.

Another WVIZ first came in 1979, when Cleveland's Fairmount Theater of the Deaf presented the play *Beauty and the Beast* in sign language. This was the first time on American television that a drama was presented in this manner. Broadcasting to the hearing-impaired audience was of great importance to WVIZ; since 1974, the station regularly presents programs with closed-captioning.

FINDING TREASURES IN CLEVELAND

Betty discovered still more local talent in the form of an unpretentious Shaker Heights couple. While they weren't musical, they were certainly entertaining. Ralph and Terry Kovel were nationally recognized antique experts. Their daily column, *Know Your Antiques*, had been syndicated in Scripps-Howard newspapers throughout the United States since the

Ralph and Terry Kovel, nationally recognized antique experts, hosted *Know Your Antiques* on WVIZ from 1969 to 1972. *Ideastream archives.*

Betty Cope with the new satellite that was installed in 1978. *From the Cleveland Plain Dealer archives.*

early 1950s. By the mid-1960s, the Kovels had also authored several books and price guides on antique silver, pottery, and furniture. In 1969, Betty approached Ralph and Terry with the prospect of hosting their own show on which they could identify and appraise antiques, and they readily accepted. He was boisterous and opinionated; she was calm and confident. Together, they were a hit. By 1972, WVIZ had produced twenty-six *Know Your Antiques* programs, which were distributed nationally and drew a wide audience. "Betty was tough as nails, but she was a good businesswoman," remembered Terry Kovel. "She was in complete control in front of a camera. But she trusted us to put together a good show. We even went out in a van and toured flea markets." Laughing, Kovel recalled, "She gave me the best advice about what to wear and what not to wear when you're on camera."

The Kovels were fixtures at the annual televised WVIZ Auctions, colorfully describing numerous antiques that attracted huge bids each year (see chapter 8, "Hey Kids, Let's Put on a Show!"). Perhaps even more importantly to Betty, they remained lifelong friends, often entertaining at each other's residences and sharing stories about collectibles (see chapter 13, "Her Legacy Lives On").

Top: A technical director is shown in the control room at WVIZ in the 1970s. *Gary Bluhm collection.*

Bottom: The exterior of WVIZ's Brookpark Road studios as it appeared in 1977. *Ideastream archives.*

The Audience Grows

As WVIZ's audience grew during the 1970s, it became necessary to improve its signal quality. A translator was added in 1978 to transmit programs to Ashtabula County. In addition, PBS was producing a record number of new programs—everything from miniseries such as *I, Claudius* and *Upstairs, Downstairs* to *Nova* and *Cosmos*. Tapes of PBS programs were no longer shipped to affiliates but rather broadcast via satellite. In July 1978, WVIZ installed its first satellite, which was funded by the CPB and federal grants. The satellite enabled Cleveland's PBS affiliate to receive an even wider variety of PBS programs for its audience.

The 1970s is remembered as a truly golden era for WVIZ as it became a prolific center of local productions. Many of its producers and directors won local Emmys for their unprecedented, high-quality, mind-expanding programs. Rather than moving earth in mines, the former tractor showroom was now moving Cleveland's minds.

8

Hey Kids, Let's Put On a Show!

There are some astounding events that occur in communities just once a year, and the citizens of those localities anxiously await and relish every moment of them. The residents of San Juan Capistrano joyously look forward to the landing of the swallows each October; Pennsylvanians anticipate the emergence of Punxsutawney Phil every February 2; even Hinkley folks look to the skies for their beloved buzzards each March. In just the same manner, northeast Ohioans sat before their television sets each spring to watch the entrance march of an enormous stuffed zebra that kicked off their favorite local entertainment show, the annual WVIZ Auction. Long before QVC, HSN, Amazon, and eBay, the Channel 25 Auction was Cleveland's own home shopping experience. For fifty years, viewers throughout northeast Ohio were treated to a barrage of local celebrity auctioneers and a treasure trove of antiques, collectibles, and household and luxury items, all for the purpose of raising funds for their public television station. Loyal Auction fans—and there were thousands of them—excitedly sat by their phones, called in their bids, checked their bids, frantically bid again if they had been outbid by another viewer, and waited seemingly forever for the announcement of the highest bids. If they were lucky enough to be the high bidder and have their names announced on TV, they could bask in their fifteen seconds of fame.

Unlike the instantaneous communication and social media fixation that dominate the twenty-first century, the WVIZ Auction years were an era of local television appreciation. Cleveland public television fans over fifty

The WVIZ Zebra promoted the Auction as the "Greatest Show on Air." *Author's collection.*

will likely reflect on that time with great fondness. It was an era when the viewing public enjoyed the originality of live local television, and Betty Cope and WVIZ rose to the occasion. Betty's experiences with the anything-can-happen live broadcasts of the Uncle Jake and Dorothy Fuldheim shows at WEWS in the 1950s certainly paved the way for her presentation of the Auction. The Auction gave her a chance to return to her live-television roots. For Betty, the Auction represented a showcase of her dedicated station staff along with the best of Cleveland's celebrities, politicians, sports figures, and newsmakers. Under Betty's leadership, there was a camaraderie among station employees, volunteers, and celebrities who joined together to put forth their best efforts and support the station. As the effervescent longtime Auction chairperson Dianne Miller recalled, "It was like a Mickey Rooney–Judy Garland musical—c'mon kids, let's put on a show!" It was a wonderful time in which the entire station—both those in front of and behind the cameras—and the whole northeast Ohio community gathered to have fun and raise money for public broadcasting.

IN THE BEGINNING

By the time that WVIZ reached the airwaves in 1965, public television auctions were standard fare for other major cities. The first fundraising auction for educational television was broadcast on KCET-TV in San Francisco in 1953. For Betty, however, the WVIZ Auction would be something uniquely *Cleveland*. With her advertising background, Betty knew the importance of television exposure for corporations. In 1968, she recruited Republic Steel and Alcoa as underwriters for the cost of broadcasting the Auction. Curtis Lee Smith, retired head of the Cleveland Chamber of Commerce, was appointed general manager of the Auction. The Women's Council of WVIZ, which formed in 1966, canvassed the community for donations. An army of volunteers led the Auction effort throughout northeast Ohio. A team of regional "captains" and "coordinators" organized the "go-getters" to solicit new donated items and gift certificates from local businesses. Men's and women's teams of go-getters competed to collect the most items.

For those who have never witnessed a WVIZ Auction, the chaos and pandemonium that accompanied this annual Cleveland rite of spring were remarkable. One-line descriptions of donated items, ranging from new household goods and artwork to antiques and collectibles, were displayed on

The *Cleveland Press* advertised the 1978 WVIZ Auction on its "TV Showtime" cover. *Author's collection*.

Mike Massa (*left*) as "King Kwickie" with one of his loyal subjects, circa 1988. *Ideastream archives*.

four separate chalkboards labeled A, B, C, and X. Auctioneers, often local celebrities, would read descriptions of the items supplied by the go-getters as the camera operators showed the items on the air. Board showings were rotated so that as bids were coming in for one board, a new board would be shown. After approximately ten minutes (or much longer for more expensive items), the previous board would "close," meaning that no more bids would be accepted for that board. A separate board, nicknamed "The Kwickie Board," was devoted solely to gift certificates for products or services. Mike Massa, announcer for WVIZ's high school sports broadcasts, brought his unique sense of humor and unmatched enthusiasm to his role as auctioneer of the Kwickie Board. On the "Tonight Board" and "Big Board," high-ticket items such as trips or cars would usually be reserved for showing during prime-time hours for maximum exposure.

While the boards were shown and items were auctioned, bid takers in the phone bank would record the bidder's information on a printed form; bid runners would then hurriedly carry those forms to the appropriate Auction table. Board markers updated bids on the boards. Other phone volunteers might call bidders to verify bids for more valuable items. After the boards closed and bids were confirmed, the same auctioneers would announce the high bidders. If items were sold at prices exceeding their declared values, floor director Frank Strnad would honk a Harpo Marx–style bicycle horn to salute the over-bidder. With nearly two hundred volunteers jammed into the small studio taking calls, running bids, marking bids, and moving cameras, boards, and tables full of items, the studio was full of a cacophony of mirth and mayhem.

The very first WVIZ Auction, advertised as the "WVIZATHON" and the "Armchair Auction," commenced on May 9, 1968, and was scheduled for three days. Over one thousand bids were taken by phone in the studio during the first hour. Dozens of wedding items, including gowns, tuxedo rentals, photographers, cakes, and flowers were successfully auctioned. Trips to Niagara Falls and the Bahamas, color TVs, and babysitting services proved to be popular with bidders. Cleveland Indians pitching legend Bob Feller sold sports memorabilia for high overbids. A quarter horse named "Go Chubby" sold for $600. After the first day on the air, so many new donated items flooded the station that the warehouse stock had doubled, and a fourth day, Sunday, May 12, was added to the schedule. By the conclusion of that very first Auction, over $50,000 was raised. Betty knew that she was on to something good for WVIZ and Cleveland.

In 1969, the WVIZ Auction was extended from four to six days. Mayor Carl Stokes was a featured auctioneer, and even more local television and radio celebrities and *Plain Dealer* columnists joined the ranks of auctioneers. World-renowned antique experts and Shaker Heights residents Ralph and Terry Kovel made their first appearance at the 1969 Auction, selling, among many other items, a Victorian tea urn, a miner's lamp, and a French wine chiller. In its second year, Channel 25 Auction earnings increased from the previous year by 50 percent to $73,000.

A first for 1970 was a preview of art and antiques held ten days before start of Auction at the Cleveland Garden Center on East Boulevard. Opening bids were made at preview. Also in 1970, numismatic items were first auctioned. An English taxicab donated by Cleveland businessman Jess Bell, owner of Bonne Bell cosmetics, drew high bids that year.

As the Auction grew in popularity, so did the number of big-ticket items and publicity stunts. In 1971, the Cuyahoga County Chrysler-Plymouth dealers donated a Duster "Twister" to the Auction. The Twister was one of its sportiest models, complete with a sunroof. The dealers and Auction program managers cooked up their biggest attention-getting scheme yet.

Radio personality Ted Lux holding an antique headboard and assisting the Kovels at an Auction during the early 1970s. *Ted Lux collection.*

As WVIZ Auction emcee, Ted Lux showed the "Tonight Board" with high-ticket items, circa 1970s. *Ted Lux collection.*

They parked the Duster on a platform of railroad ties on the roof of a fourteen-story food distribution terminal building above Interstate 71, where it could be seen by passing highway motorists. Then they recruited Ted Lux, the all-night disc jockey from WKYC radio, to broadcast from the top of the warehouse and advertise the car during the entire Auction. "When I first got the assignment, I was not happy about the show. But it was a fun experience," recalled Lux, who had only moved to Cleveland two years prior. While spotlights shone on the car at night, "People would honk their car horns and flash their lights on I-71 when I asked them to do so. It was an ego booster," laughed the retired deejay. The engineers' union required that an engineer be present for the duration of the assignment. "Buzz Buzinski got stuck up there with me, and we lived in a trailer on the roof for that entire week. I didn't shave, so that people could see that I was up there the whole time. The best part was the fantastic food that they brought up from the warehouse," Lux remembered. The Duster finally sold for $3,600 (about a tenth of its value today) to the owner of a trucking company.

According to Lux, the only problem with living on a warehouse roof for a week was "there was no bathroom. We had call up a freight elevator to take us down to a restroom." But often, especially during Auction broadcasts,

Ted Lux during his infamous stint as rooftop auctioneer with the 1971 Plymouth Duster. *Ted Lux collection*.

there wasn't time to wait for an elevator and come back again and be ready on camera. "The roof was gigantic, so we just had to stand behind something to go," remembered Lux. "One night after the Auction signed off, we went and did our business. Right when I finished, the elevator door opened, and out stepped Betty Cope and Mary Zunt, who was a Cleveland City Councilwoman. I just about flipped!" Betty simply wanted check on Lux's welfare and show her appreciation for his efforts. "She truly cared about the people who worked for her and helped to put together the Auction." Lux went on to work as an emcee for the Auction for another forty years.

Another memorable event of the '71 Auction was a visit from British film and stage actor Arthur Treacher, who is best remembered as the P.G. Wodehouse character "Jeeves" the valet and later as the reserved sidekick on Merv Griffin's afternoon talk show. At the time, the actor was a spokesman for the fast-food chain Arthur Treacher's Fish and Chips, which provided nourishment for hungry volunteers for the entire week of the Auction. (n.b., Treacher never publicly confirmed or denied financial involvement in the restaurant chain.) Engineer Larry Tressler remembered, "Although fried fish and chips are very good, we learned that you cannot eat that greasy stuff every day and stay well. By the third day, most of the crew experienced not just stomach discomfort, but explosive diarrhea. If you were there… you would never forget it. It's amazing the things you remember most about Auction Week."

The Auction Grows Up

By 1972, a format of pre-Auction organization had begun to take shape; it was a format that would be followed for decades to come. Go-getter kickoff meetings were held in March of that year, and regional captains and coordinators kept tabs on incoming donations. The planning efforts paid off, as Auction proceeds climbed steadily thereafter. In just a few years, the Auction had become a favorite with the northeast Ohio viewing public. "The Auction has a carnival atmosphere as auctioneers and volunteers get caught up in the spirit," wrote Raymond Hart, former TV editor of the *Plain Dealer*. "The fun and games flavor of the studio is conveyed to the viewer." In 1978, Betty remarked, "About the third year [1971], we realized that we had a hit on our hands, not just a fundraiser. We realized that people were addicted to it—alternative television at its best."

While some viewers registered their complaints with the station for missing regular programming, Betty defended the Auction as a necessary part of running the station. "The Auction is entertainment unto itself," she said in 1976. "The fact that it also brings in 300K plus for future programming has to add up that the Auction pretty much makes sense. For one chaotic week, non-commercial WVIZ turns commercial to raise the bulk of the funding for the next 51 weeks of commercial-free programming." It should be noted that WVIZ never preempted daytime educational programs for the Auction. Clearly, Betty remained committed to her goal of education, even during the station's largest fundraiser.

The televised Auction expanded to eight days in 1973; a ninth day was added two years later. WVIZ drew Auction underwriting sponsorships from some of Cleveland's largest companies, including Sherwin-Williams, Eaton Corporation, American Greetings, Reliance Electric, Alcan Aluminum, Tremco, and Standard Oil (SOHIO). These companies remained sponsors for nearly all of the Auction years. Several Cleveland corporations even donated stock packages for the Big Boards of the Auction, which were often sold for high overbids.

As a tribute (or perhaps a favor) to their famous alumnus, WEWS in the mid-1970s began to simulcast thirty minutes of the first Sunday afternoon of the Auction. Channel 5 personalities served as auctioneers, and expensive Big Board items were often showcased. The brief broadcast on the commercial station served WVIZ well as it provided some helpful publicity to a more varied audience. The tradition of the WEWS simulcast continued throughout the history of the Auction.

THE AUCTION "STARS"

While many local celebrities, politicians, and other noteworthy citizens often served as auctioneers, including Governor George Voinovich in 1991, there were perennial favorites as well. Ralph and Terry Kovel's on-camera repartee—with one often correcting the other about the valued merchandise—made for highly entertaining broadcasts. For nearly forty years, the Kovels (and Terry alone for another nine years after Ralph's death) shared their vast knowledge of antiques and auctioned fabulous Victorian furniture, colorful Depression glassware, one-of-a-kind early jewelry, clocks, rare porcelains, and a myriad of old treasures to WVIZ fans across northeast

We're putting our money on a Zebra.

No ordinary Zebra is this. Specifically, it's the WVIZ-TV 25 mascot for the 1978 WVIZ auction that will be on view from Saturday, May 13 through Sunday, May 21. This annual fund raiser for WVIZ makes possible non-commercial, public television in the Cleveland area.

As a business member of the Cleveland community, Reliance Electric has an on-going interest in the cultural, as well as the economic health of Cleveland. So, Reliance is putting its money behind WVIZ and the WVIZ Zebra on May 14 by underwriting the air time and production expenses on that day of the auction.

Put your money, and your attention on WVIZ-TV, along with the thousands of viewers, industrial companies and merchants from the Cleveland area who support and encourage the efforts of WVIZ. All of us have a lot riding on the WVIZ Zebra.

Page 29

The Cleveland Press, May 12, 1978

RELIANCE ELECTRIC

Reliance Electric advertisement showing its support of the 1978 WVIZ Auction as shown in the *Cleveland Press* TV Showtime guide. *Author's collection.*

1979 WVIZ AUCTION
May 12-20.

TUNE IN...
and get the picture.

Tune in, and take part in the 1979 WVIZ Auction, May 12-20, and help insure a bright future for non-commercial, public television in Cleveland.

Reliance Electric is doing its part to support WVIZ by sponsoring one full day of the Auction on Sunday, May 13.

We hope you'll join in the fun, and do your part, too.

Tune in. Call in. Phone 621-2525. Help keep WVIZ alive and well, and living in the homes of everyone in Greater Cleveland.

Get the picture?

Page 29

The Cleveland Press, May 11, 1979

A-1418

Reliance Electric advertisement showing its support of the 1979 WVIZ Auction as shown in the *Cleveland Press* TV Showtime guide. *Author's collection.*

Ohio. Viewers were treated to tutorials in history just by watching the Kovels. But their personas—he often vocal and opinionated and she quiet and even-tempered—were the main reason that viewers tuned in to the Auction. "The Kovels were Cleveland's version of the Bickersons," remembered retired WVIZ engineer Gary Bluhm.

"Ralph was a very likeable guy with a great sense of humor," recalled Ted Lux, "but he was also very frank, and he didn't always remember to turn off his microphone after the antique board was sold. One night, as he and Terry were walking away after selling their board, Ralph could be heard saying on the air, 'I don't know who in their right mind would buy that piece of crap.' Mind you, he used other colorful language. The whole studio cracked up, and a technician ran over to Ralph to turn off his mike. It was hilarious."

Through their work at WVIZ, Ralph and Terry developed a genuinely close friendship with Betty. One year, knowing Betty took all Auction donations very seriously, Ralph decided to play a trick on her. He approached a clever artist to decorate an earthenware bowl in the same manner as Viktor Schreckengost's famous "Jazz" pattern. At an Auction preview meeting, Ralph proudly displayed the fake bowl on a stand and began describing WVIZ's incredible good fortune in obtaining the "priceless" donation.

Betty Cope relaxing on an antique loveseat with the Kovels in the background, circa 1978. *Henry family collection.*

Top: Ralph and Terry Kovel, world-renowned antique experts, presented antiques at the WVIZ Auction for nearly four decades. *Author's collection*.

Bottom: Betty and Carol Bosley displayed their zebra-themed shirts at a 1970s Auction. *Carter Edman collection*.

The Cleveland Press

May 11-18, 1979

TV SHOWTIME

Art expert Carol Bosley promoted the WVIZ Auction on a 1979 *Cleveland Press* TV Showtime cover. *Author's collection*.

Apparently, the contemporary artist did an amazing job of re-creating the classic bowl. As Ralph enthusiastically touted the features of the famed artwork, he pretended to accidentally knock over the phony bowl, sending it crashing to the floor. "Of course, Betty freaked out," laughed Ted Lux. "Finally Ralph explained that the broken bowl wasn't a real Schreckengost work of art. Ralph was probably the only person who would have gotten away with playing that joke on Betty."

The Kovels also demonstrated their deep affection for Betty during the Auction. One year, a black teacup poodle was being auctioned. Always a dog lover, Betty immediately fell in love with the pup. The antique experts took note of Betty's reaction and, joining forces with Betty's sister, Janet, phoned in an exceptionally high anonymous bid from one of the station offices. At the end of the evening, the Kovels presented an astonished Betty with her new pet, which she promptly named "Luv." For years, Betty brought the toy poodle to work with her at the Brookpark Road studios.

Carol Bosley, a teacher in the Mentor School District, began working for WVIZ in the 1960s as an instructor on televised educational programs that were broadcast to schools and colleges throughout northeast Ohio. She also produced several programs for the station, including the *Ohio Stories* history series and the Emmy Award–winning *Get Ready for the Cleveland Orchestra*. Among WVIZ viewers, Carol is perhaps best remembered as the Art Auctioneer for the annual Auction. Her passion for arts and culture from around the world was reflected in her enthusiasm on the Auction's "A" board. Carol auctioned a multitude of media to Cleveland viewers, including oil paintings, watercolors, "whiskey paintings," sculptures, photographs, fabrics, and pottery. Her descriptions of the art she sold were much like art lessons in themselves. Through it all, Carol took a great deal of ribbing from the station technicians. While auctioning nude art one year, she maintained her composure despite heckling from all the men in the studio.

Knowing the importance of visual presentation to sell valuable artwork, Carol worked closely with the Auction producers and camera crew. Longtime art board table captain Laurel Kest remembered, "She coordinated the art board schedule and sequence of items. She trained the cameramen to zoom in on particular details of the artwork. She even trained me how to hold the artwork at the best angle for the cameras." Carol's contributions to the WVIZ Auction were invaluable. "Her depth of knowledge on art was unmatched," reflected Laurel. "It was such a loss to the Auction when she retired."

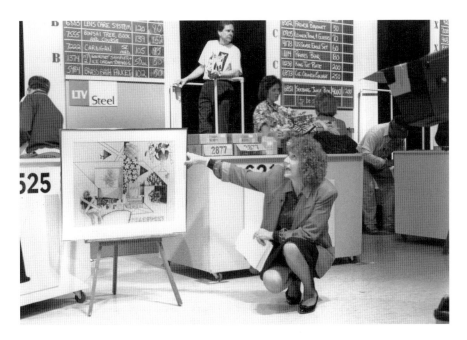

Carol Bosley (*crouching*) pointing out essential details of a painting that was up for bids at the 1990 WVIZ Auction. *Carter Edman collection.*

Real-time artwork was featured on the 1990 and 1991 Auctions. Shaker Heights artist Jack Loney illustrated the hubbub of the studio floor while the Auction was underway. The finished painting was sold on the final day of the 1990 Auction. In 1991, to mark the success of the PBS Civil War Series, Loney painted a watercolor of Johnson Island in Sandusky Bay, where Confederate soldiers were imprisoned. The original and three prints were auctioned on the final Sunday that year.

While not all of the artwork presented on the Auction had universal appeal with viewers, there was one item that proved so popular that it brought up to 200 percent overbids. Marie Nyland of Olmsted Falls began creating whimsical glazed terra-cotta planters of bears, squirrels, and other animals in the late 1980s. She donated a few of them to the WVIZ Auction, and they caught on like wildfire. After a few years and numerous overbids, Marie started donating a planter for each night of the Auction. Whenever a Nyland planter was shown, phone lines were always jammed.

Perhaps the most colorful auctioneer came in the unlikely form of a Cleveland tax accountant. In 1969, Myron Xenos was the high bidder on a certificate for "Be an Auctioneer on WVIZ." Besides being a fervent

Above: Carol Bosley describing artwork in front of a camera in a busy studio during an Auction, circa 1970. *Carter Edman collection.*

Opposite: Betty posing with psychedelic art that was donated to the Auction, circa 1969. *CSU Memory Project.*

philatelist and member of the Numismatic Bibliomania Society, Myron was an expert on just about any sort of collectible. From first day cover stamps to Madame Alexander dolls, from Hummel figurines to rare coins, his knowledge and unique sense of humor entertained Auction viewers for decades. The vast array of collectibles that were donated to the Auction was astounding. Dental chairs, animation cells, signed newspaper cartoons, Avon perfume bottles, radio and television tubes, gumball machines, refinished fire extinguishers, and the ever-popular telephone booths were just some of the items that Myron presented on the Auction. Even WVIZ Auction memorabilia such as limited-edition Auction clocks, thermometers, mugs, and stained-glass window hangings became sought-after collectibles. With a plethora of trivia and puns about each and every collectible up for bids, Myron kept the studio and viewers in stitches.

Some of the most memorable collectibles sold by Myron on the Collectible board were posters of burlesque dancers from the long-closed Roxy Theater. "It seemed like every year for six or seven years straight, Myron was auctioning off Roxy Theater posters," recalled retired WGAR deejay Jim Szymanski. "I once asked him if they were real or reprints. Myron said that they were real. He said that the reason that we saw them for so many years was because guys would buy the posters, and their wives wouldn't like them, and would make them donate them back again. So the same posters were shown year after year!"

A Veritable Cornucopia of Items Up for Bids

Besides antiques, art, and collectibles, just about anything and everything was sold at the WVIZ Auction: jewelry, lawn equipment, appliances, hand-made quilts and afghans, bird feeders, lamps, bicycles, clocks, pool tables, home décor, assorted gift baskets, and tons of gift certificates for local attractions, restaurants, products, and services. A personal bagpipe and drum performance by the Cleveland Kiltie band was a favorite on the Tonight Board for years. Even the Cleveland Metroparks donated animal dung to be sold as "Zoo Poo," which proved to be a highly sought-after item.

Back in the 1970s, before animal protection laws were enacted, ponies were sold nearly every night during the Auction. Puppies, a pair of watch roosters, and a cow were donated by a local farm in 1975. That year, animal lovers kept the station's phones busy with fast and furious bidding on these creatures.

Right: Numismatic expert Myron Xenos was the collectibles auctioneer at WVIZ for nearly fifty years, pictured here in 1996. *Wayne Homren collection.*

Below: Myron Xenos in his element, evaluating rare coins, circa 1980s. *Wayne Homren collection.*

High-profile sports figures started donating to the Auction as well; Muhammad Ali donated autographed boxing gloves, Arnold Palmer provided a week's stay with unlimited golfing at his Bay Hill Club in Florida, and Ozzie Newsome brought one of his Cleveland Browns football uniforms to the Auction. Perhaps the most expensive offering from the world of sports came from George Steinbrenner, who donated a yearling filly to the 1977 Auction.

Over the years, the WVIZ Auction offered hundreds of items to travel enthusiasts, who were especially excited to bid on trips to Mexico, the Bahamas, New York, Israel, England, Las Vegas, Denmark, Disney World, and the Virgin Islands, just to name a few. Airlines donated certificates for thousands of miles of airfare, which usually went for large overbids. For land travel, Cleveland area auto dealerships continued the tradition that started with the infamous '71 Duster. They provided new cars to the Auction nearly every year from the 1970s to the mid-80s.

For some special events, the Auction provided one-stop shopping. "I had a very successful time at the Auction the year I got married," remembered Larry Tressler. "I was the successful bidder on my share of wedding services. I got our wedding cake, photographer, printed invitations, and some business cards for my part time job from the Auction that year. The Auction studio crew always had one extra 'floating' crew member to take over if someone needed a bathroom break or just a short rest. Making a bid from the studio was frowned upon because it wouldn't be fair to the bidders calling from home. So when I saw an item that I could use, I would ask the extra crew person to take over while I went into a nearby office and called the Auction, just like any other viewer. I'm still married to the same wonderful lady after 50+ years."

The Auction Mom

Volunteers were the backbone of the Auction. One even rose through the ranks to become the "Auction Mom." Dianne Miller began volunteering as a go-getter in 1983 and graduated to the south regional coordinator position. She also worked on the scheduling committee for several years. Finally, in 1990, Betty hired Dianne to fill the role of Auction chairperson, a position she held until 2003. "During my second Auction in 1992, flyers were going to be printed to solicit donors. My volunteer assistant, Jim Donahue and

The always-smiling Dianne Miller (*at right, shown here with husband Dave*) served with tremendous dedication as WVIZ Auction chairperson for thirteen years. *Dianne and Dave Miller*.

I, each proofread the written copy. When the flyers came back from the printers, we were horrified to see that the zip code for the station was listed as 44143 instead of 44134. Also the wrong dates were listed for the Auction. Betty had high expectations. She was direct and wanted to know how we were going to fix the problem. Jim painstakingly fixed the errors by hand on each of the two thousand brochures!"

Betty believed in presenting quality television programming, and the Auction was no exception. The preparation for the Auction broadcast was intense, and it required the utmost dedication on the part of the WVIZ staff and volunteers. Dianne Miller recalled that Betty had unwritten rules for Auction managers. "With Betty, there was no cutting corners. She wanted it done the right way. During the Auction, there were to be no weddings, First Communions, graduations, no moving, and you couldn't have sex, and you couldn't die." For many years, in fact, Dianne stayed in the building throughout the entire Auction. "My predecessor told me to keep a supply of tampons and panty hose in my desk drawer for the Auction," laughed Dianne.

Sherrill Paul Witt, owner of Trolley Tours of Cleveland, served as a Kwickie Board auctioneer for many years. *From the* Cleveland Plain Dealer *archives*.

Monumental Technical Efforts

Putting on the big show demanded hundreds of engineering hours for the studio setup. "The annual Auction was a real love-hate situation with the crew," said retired engineer Larry Tressler. "It was something exciting to look forward to because it only came around once a year. But it was a royal pain in the rear." Remembered retired engineer Dick Barnick, "For two weeks before the Auction and two weeks after, it seemed like nothing else was getting done!" Fellow retiree Gary Bluhm echoed the sentiments of the entire engineering staff as he recalled, "We re-lit the entire studio, moved cameras, assembled the phone banks for the bid-takers, hauled tables and huge boards, and moved large items from the donation warehouse to the sold warehouse. Then after the Auction, we had to dismantle everything. It was hard work, but we had a blast." The only problem, as Barnick recalled, was that all other programming was put on hold during the Auction. "Work on shows like *Newsdepth* and other daytime shows had to be postponed until the Auction was over. Then we had to record all the nighttime network programs so that they could be shown after the Auction."

Betty—The Best Party Hostess

In all respects, Betty truly cared for the Auction volunteers. She was always concerned about having sufficient meal provisions, stating, "An army of volunteers marches on its stomach." Dianne recalled, "At the end of each late-night shift—which sometimes was about two o'clock in the morning—it was Betty's idea that she and I should stand by the front exit and say 'Thank you' and 'Good night' to each and every volunteer as he or she was leaving." According to Laurel Kest, "Betty really wanted to know all of the volunteers. She made a point of learning everyone's names."

Betty was extremely detail-oriented about everything—even checking the on-air copy for big-ticket items, setting up items on Auction tables, and working with the accountants. She threw herself into every aspect of the Auction. "In the late 1980s, there was an incident that was just quintessential Betty," remembered Dianne. "We received a donation of a pot-bellied pig. Well, the pig got excited when the cameras and lights were fixed on him, and he pooped right on the air. Betty just got down on the floor and cleaned it up with some paper towels. It was her party, so she just did what she had to do!"

Parma resident Terry Manke worked in the station's traffic office, keeping station time logs during the early 1970s. She remembered one spring when torrential rains fell and began to flood the garage behind the studio, where donations of huge expensive antique breakfronts and cabinets were stored. "The water was coming in so fast it actually blew off the grate of the drain in the garage," said Terry. "A group of us got brooms and pushed all the water out to keep it away from the furniture. Then Betty came back there and helped to clean up the water. Her attitude was always 'You do what you need to do.' It was just that kind of atmosphere under Betty."

Betty viewed the volunteer positions of bid-checkers and bid confirmation workers very seriously. Her brother-in-law, businessman Fred Henry, was one of the original bid-checkers in 1968. "Everyone who worked those two jobs had to be 'Betty-approved,' remembers Dianne. Those who took on these roles were richly rewarded for their dedication. One year, Dianne's husband, Dave Miller, worked bid confirmation until 3:00 a.m. Dave taught in Parma City Schools, where classes were scheduled to begin the next day at 8:00 a.m. "I jokingly asked Betty if she would write an excuse for Dave for the next day—and she actually did! She composed a hand-written note on a WVIZ letterhead stating that Dave had performed an extremely important service for the community, and asked the principal to excuse him from work that day. And she signed it!"

Moreover, Betty took complete responsibility when things didn't go right on the air. A memorable stunt that was conceived in the late 1980s was the "Auction Game." Young executive producer Mark Rosenberger, dressed in a zebra-patterned tuxedo jacket, presented various items on the air and invited viewers to phone in the correct total dollar value of the grouping. The game was akin to the 1960s *Price Is Right* mail-in sweepstakes. "The only problem with the Auction Game was that the phone number shown on the screen was the *wrong number*. So wrong, in fact, it was the number for a phone sex line! Two of the digits in the phone number were interposed. The staff only realized the mistake after angry viewers called the station office," remembered Rosenberger, now chief content officer for WVIZ Ideastream. "As soon as she learned of the error, Betty went in front of the cameras and apologized profusely to the viewing audience." Needless to say, the Auction Game was not brought back for a second year.

A Family Tradition

The final Sunday of each Auction was always formal, with studio workers and auctioneers wearing donated tuxedos and evening gowns. The most highly valued art and antiques were always reserved for auctioning on Sunday evening. In the early 1970s, Auction staff and volunteers started a tradition that celebrated their camaraderie. Following the final Sunday's Auction, which most years went off the air sometime after 2:00 a.m. on Monday, Auction staff and volunteers held the "TOPPY" awards presentation. The awards were jokingly named after TOPS cola, a local soda pop that was donated in huge quantities for Auction volunteer consumption. The TOPPYs were awarded to the auctioneer who made the funniest on-air faux pas. Volunteers and staff who managed to stay awake roared while viewing film clips of Auction bloopers. As if they did not want the Auction experience to end, the group then proceeded to a local Denny's for a hearty breakfast.

The conviviality enjoyed by the Auction co-workers was such that numerous dignitaries, on-air personalities, and volunteers returned year after year. Many felt that the Auction was like an annual family reunion that provided an opportunity to reminisce, laugh, and catch up on the latest news. In essence, many regarded one another as family with a job to do—to help their esteemed station manager raise money for their favorite television station. Said Laurel Kest, "Betty cared about everyone who worked the Auction, and we all worked hard for her."

While Betty considered the station employees and Auction volunteers as her family, her own family was just as deeply involved in the annual fundraiser. For many years, Betty's sister, Janet Henry, served as hostess to the celebrity auctioneers, greeting them and welcoming them to the green room before they went on the air. "Janet was such a warm person and made everyone feel comfortable," Jim Szymanski reminisced. "After she passed away, they asked me if I would fill in that role, so I did that for one year. I was honored to be asked." Subsequently, Janet's daughter Heidi Henry Cregar took over the task of greeting and serving refreshments to the auctioneers. Heidi remembers that as a tribute to her beloved late sister, Betty would say softly under her breath, "Thanks, Jan," at the end of the Sunday night Auction proceedings.

Betty's nieces and nephews played an integral role in Auction proceedings for decades. "We literally did everything, especially at the beginning," remembered niece Chris Henry. "Besides greeting the auctioneers with Mom, we made up the boards, worked as table assistants,

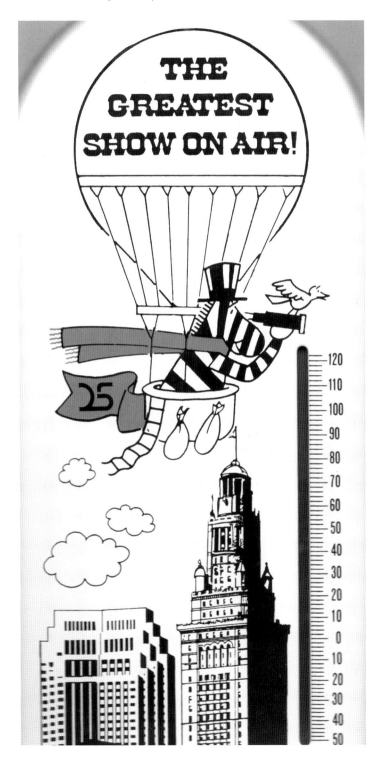

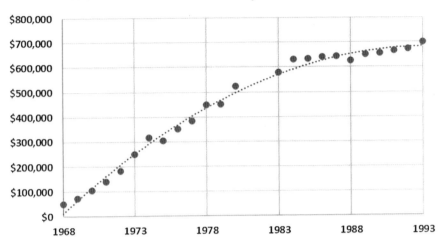

WVIZ Auction Proceeds by Year 1968 - 1993

Above: WVIZ Auction proceeds are shown by year from 1968 to 1993, which was Betty Cope's tenure. *Author's collection.*

Opposite: This collectible enameled steel sign with thermometer commemorated the 1988 WVIZ Auction. *Author's collection.*

scheduled workers, anything that was needed. The boys [the Henry brothers] worked on bid confirmation with our dad." "It took over our world and we happily embraced it," said Heidi Henry Cregar. "During the summers, Betty would have a party at her cabin for all of the Auction chairpersons and captains. We [the nieces and nephews] would serve everybody. She was just that generous."

For the twenty-five years that the Auction was held under Betty's leadership, the annual televised Auction was the largest fundraiser for WVIZ. During this time, the station on the whole realized an average of 70 to 80 percent of the retail value of its auctioned items, which was higher than the earnings of most other cities. Throughout Betty's tenure, Cleveland's public TV fundraiser was, per capita, the second-highest-grossing Auction in the United States; the top spot belonged to San Francisco. For this reason, Betty was enormously proud of the devotion of the Auction volunteers and supporters. Betty certainly did her part: the success of the Auction meant so much to her that she even gave up her paid vacation time during the annual televised fundraiser. "She didn't want her salary to be deducted from the proceeds," remembered Laurel Kest. (The continued success of the Auction during that era is demonstrated in the graph aboove.)

Auction proceeds were poured directly back into the station for equipment upgrades such as the purchase of a full-color mobile unit with three cameras for broadcasts of high school football and basketball, as well as the Cleveland Orchestra and ballet performances. Another major post-Auction purchase was a new video switcher, a device that selects between multiple incoming video signals from various sources and directs one of those signals to a single output, such as a display. The new equipment required tens of thousands of dollars in capital expenditures. Improvements to production equipment meant that the technical assets of the public television station would compete with those of commercial stations. Enhanced technical capabilities would also boost the production quality of WVIZ's programs.

Not only did the annual Auction build a financially successful, state-of-the-art public television station, but it also built thriving, long-lasting friendships among its volunteers and station workers. From all standpoints, the Auction was the foundation that supported the house of the WVIZ family.

9

The 1980s

Still Great Quality, but Creativity Gives Way to Caution and Criticism

W hile the 1970s were a decade of flourishing creativity of WVIZ productions, the 1980s were met with a more cautious, financially conservative approach. Near the end of the decade, Betty's conservatism in production faced harsh criticism from local newspaper writers. Nevertheless, the quality of WVIZ productions remained as high as ever, and local viewers remained loyal to their public television station. First and foremost a teacher, Betty focused on bringing only the best educational and informative programs to her beloved northeast Ohio viewers.

WVIZ TAKES ON MORE HISTORICALLY SOCIAL ISSUES

Always socially conscious, Betty and her staff offered many shows that brought historically significant issues to the forefront. In January 1980, Jewish Community Theater director Reuben Silver hosted *But Still We Remember*, which presented a display of artistic expressions of enslaved African Americans from the Cleveland Museum of Art. Zelma George and the William Appling Singers collaborated on the February 1983 WVIZ special *A Joyful Noise*. The historical and cultural meanings of African American spirituals were celebrated in this program through the presentation of moving songs and readings. An hour-long program in April 1985 took a hard look at the progress of Cleveland's desegregation program. *Desegregation: Making the Grade?* raised tough questions about the effectiveness of busing students in the city.

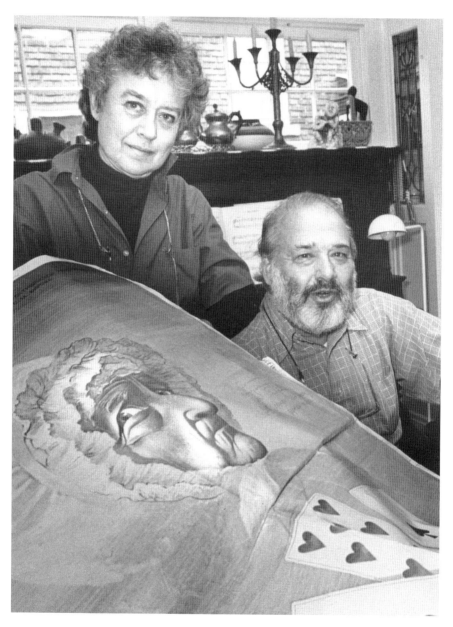

Dorothy and Reuben Silver, directors of Cleveland's Jewish Community Theater, produced educational and entertaining programs for WVIZ. *Author's collection.*

In 1983, Zelma George and the William Appling Singers presented *A Joyful Noise* on WVIZ. *Author's collection.*

Edward Asner narrated the poignant WVIZ production *Tomorrow Came Much Later*, which documented the travels of Cleveland Heights High School students with Holocaust survivor Bertha Lautman to a World War II concentration camp where the Nazis had interred her. They also visited Vienna, where the students interviewed famed Nazi hunter Simon Wiesenthal. The journey was ultimately uplifting, as the group traveled to Israel, where Lautman felt she had been reborn following her liberation from the camp.

My First Hundred Years was a WVIZ-produced dramatic television special on aging. Naomi Feil, a nationally recognized gerontologist, starred in a televised play in which she portrayed all of life's stages from birth to old age. Working with the studio audience, Feil presented the most effective means of dealing with the mental aspects of aging while she revealed the wisdom that comes with old age. The program won the Corporation for Public Broadcasting's Best Program of the Year Award for 1983.

On a 1987 program titled *Fabric*, journalist Laurence Elder (later a nationally syndicated radio host) probed the issues surrounding the childcare industry. Elder interviewed pediatric medical experts and local childcare providers, discussing a variety of opinions on the matter.

Four of northeast Ohio's unconventional yet successful educational courses were featured in the March 1989 WVIZ special *Learning: Local Innovations*. Creative writing on computers, scholarships in escrow, and courses taught by satellite in Strongsville and Akron schools were just some of the subjects covered in this show.

Gerontologist Naomi Feil portrayed all ages of human life in *My First Hundred Years* on WVIZ. The show won a CPB Best Program award in 1983. *Author's collection.*

ALWAYS SHOWCASING THE LOCAL ARTS

In 1981, WVIZ presented a one-hour compilation of vignettes from the Dobama Kids' Playwriting Festival. Hosted by Dobama Theater founder Marilyn Bianchi, this Emmy Award–winning program highlighted students' various cultural experiences. Also that year, WVIZ's *Signature* provided a unique platform for local poets, pundits, and playwrights to present their thoughts to the Cleveland television audience, each in his or her own unique way.

Baldwin-Wallace College's Fiftieth Annual Bach Festival was shown by WVIZ in the spring of 1983. The sacred oratorio "St. Matthew Passion," performed by the college's orchestra and choir, was simulcast with WCLV radio and broadcast on other PBS stations throughout the country.

Reflections of Reality in Japanese Art was a 1983 WVIZ production that displayed the Asian treasures in the Cleveland Museum of Art. The program, which illustrated "Oriental" paintings, ceramics, and sculptures, was the last major exhibition under Dr. Sherman Lee before his retirement.

The concept of an orchestra as one big musical instrument was presented in WVIZ's *A Musical Encounter in Cleveland*. Members of the Cleveland Institute of Music Youth Orchestra performed numerous pieces with the intention of increasing children's appreciation of classical music.

Dr. Sherman Lee, director of the Cleveland Museum of Art, presented *Reflections of Reality in Japanese Art* on WVIZ (1983). *Author's collection.*

Local television news anchor and music lover Leon Bibb and WCPN radio's Chris Columbi teamed up to host *One Hundred Years of Jazz* on WVIZ in November 1985. Classic recordings and archival photos were combined with studio jazz band performances for a one-of-a-kind celebration of a purely American art form.

In early 1988, WVIZ continued its tradition of bringing local musical performances into the homes of its viewers. Blending folk, pop, and sacred music, *Ann Mortifee in Concert* recorded the Canadian singer-songwriter's show from Cleveland's Hanna Theater.

THE EMMYS KEEP COMING: TRULY MEMORABLE WVIZ SPECIALS

In December 1985, WVIZ presented M*argaret Bourke-White: The Right Place at the Right Time*, which chronicled the legacy of the famous photographer, who began her esteemed career photographing steel mills in Cleveland. The program was so well received that it earned its producers a local Emmy.

WVIZ's 1985 special, *A Musical Encounter in Cleveland*, featured the Cleveland Institute of Music Youth Orchestra, shown here with conductor Dung Kwak. *Author's collection.*

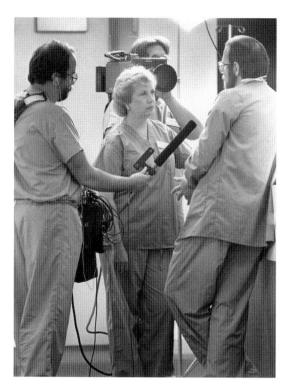

M.R. Berger interviewed Cleveland Clinic heart transplant surgeons for *Out of Tragedy Comes Triumph: A Medi-Scene Special Report*, which broke new ground for WVIZ programming in 1986. *Author's collection.*

Another Emmy Award winner for WVIZ was *Out of Tragedy Comes Triumph: A Medi-Scene Special Report* which actually documented a heart transplant surgery at the Cleveland Clinic in 1986. The program broke new ground in broadcasting as it followed a twenty-six-year-old patient from his initial diagnosis through the transplant procedure, recovery, and six-month post-procedure follow-up. The Ohio Educational Broadcasters' Association also awarded WVIZ for this significant documentary.

A monthly hour-long magazine show titled *Dimension* debuted on WVIZ in January 1987. Described by the station as a "profile of Northeast Ohio's people, pursuits, and peccadilloes," the program won a local Emmy in 1988.

Local Educational Shows for Viewers of All Ages

The educational program *Kinetics Karnival* featured physics lessons from Dr. Jearl Walker, a colorful professor at Cleveland State University. Noted for his book *The Flying Circus of Physics*, Walker demonstrated various physics principles by lying on a bed of nails, walking barefoot over hot coals, pouring liquid nitrogen in his mouth, and sticking his hand in a bath of molten lead. His thirty-minute program was distributed to PBS stations nationwide for classroom instruction and earned an Emmy in 1982.

Other locally produced programs provided prime-time education to northeast Ohio viewers. WVIZ's 1988 offering *The Underground Zoo* was hosted by local radio personality Bob Fuller. The show provided a fascinating behind-the-scenes look at exotic animal care, feeding, and maintenance at the Cleveland Metroparks Zoo.

Presented by Reuben Silver, *The Cuyahoga Valley Trilogy Special* in the April 1989 installment of *Dimension* focused on the history of the Cuyahoga River Valley and the use of the Ohio Canal and the Cuyahoga Valley Railroad. This special spawned renewed interest in the conservancy of one of northeast Ohio's historic and natural gems.

Dr. Jearl Walker, professor of physics at Cleveland State University, hosted the innovative *Kinetics Karnival* program on WVIZ, which earned an Emmy in 1982. *Cleveland State University.*

In *Race to the Moon*, shown in July 1989, WVIZ marked the twentieth anniversary of the Apollo 11 moon landing. Jacqui Bishop presented a retrospective of the Cleveland NASA Lewis Research Center's contributions to the space program.

For public television, the early 1980s experienced an upsurge in do-it-yourself Saturday afternoon programming. WVIZ catered to Clevelanders' interests with *Home Again*, which was hosted by Jim Larue. Beginning in March 1981, the series presented the step-by-step process of the total rehabilitation of a Bessemer Avenue house over a period of thirteen weeks. In early 1982, host Shirley Adams instructed would-be seamstresses with her sewing program on WVIZ titled *The Needle and the Eye*.

During another thirteen weeks in 1988, local gourmet chef Suzie Heller presented *Cooksmart* on WVIZ. Heller selected and prepared meals with ingredients native to northeast Ohio. Julia Child and Jacques Pépin were featured as special guests on two episodes of the series.

Maury's Market, a series produced by WVIZ in the fall of 1989, followed local produce merchant Maury Feren as he toured specialty food markets in various Cleveland neighborhoods. Feren also invited chefs of various ethnicities to demonstrate preparation of cultural foods.

Perhaps the greatest success of WVIZ in the 1980s was the production of *Kovels on Collecting* which brought antique experts Ralph and Terry Kovel back to public television. Beginning in October 1987, the Shaker Heights couple hosted a thirteen-part series in which they shared their expertise in locating and appraising antiques and collectibles. The show was broadcast in more than one hundred PBS markets across the country. It was quite a feather in the cap of WVIZ and earned the station another local Emmy.

Kovels on Collecting, produced by WVIZ in 1987, featured antiques experts Ralph and Terry Kovel. The program was shown in over one hundred PBS markets. *Author's collection.*

WHY STAY LOCAL?

While WVIZ's original productions of the 1980s were lauded by both viewers and critics, local newspaper writers began asking such questions as "Why keep it to ourselves? Why doesn't WVIZ go national with more programs, like WGBH, WNET, and WQED? Why doesn't Betty Cope make WVIZ a national star, too?" When confronted by *Plain Dealer* staff writer Becky Freligh about the matter, Betty responded. "The only people I've heard asking why we haven't done more national programming are media people." Citing a station member survey, Betty further added, "Viewers love us. These are the people we want telling us what to do." Freligh, however, claimed that "critics charge that WVIZ has been an underdeveloped, near-invisible resource; specifically that the station hasn't done enough to showcase Cleveland's social concerns and cultural treasures in original productions, or to find the money to do so." Freligh put the blame squarely on Betty's conservative management style.

In any public television station, funding is always the major obstacle to producing marketable programs. Before creating any national programs, stations must finance the production through corporate underwriting, government grants, or commitments from other PBS stations to purchase the shows. Producing an underfunded program or exceeding a station's budget could risk depletion of a station's operating funds. A case in point was Los Angeles's KCET, which experienced significant overruns while making *Cosmos* in the late 1970s. The station nearly went bankrupt during this time and didn't get out of the financial hole until the mid-1980s.

While quality shows like *Cooksmart, Fabric,* and *Dimension* held much promise and might have enjoyed a national audience, the budget for continued production just wasn't there. WVIZ's *Medi-Scene,* according to Freligh, was "a case of blown opportunity." The critically acclaimed health science program dwindled from a weekly to a monthly show. Host M.R. Berger, a former nurse, stated that she couldn't hire assistants to work on the program because she was told there was no money. Apparently, health care institutions offered to underwrite the program, but WVIZ refused it. Betty and her staff were concerned that the underwriters from local hospital systems might threaten the editorial integrity of the contents of the subject and possibly set a commercial tone.

The task of finding underwriting from Cleveland's business community was becoming more difficult. By the mid-1980s, the steel industry in the United States was facing stiff competition from foreign imports. Many northeast Ohio manufacturing companies suffered losses, which forced layoffs. Corporations were adopting more "lean management" styles that were directed at reducing the bottom line and were less concerned with sponsoring nonprofit organizations. Moreover, as WVIZ sought corporate funding, it also faced stiff competition from local arts organizations, including the Great Lakes Theater Festival, the Fairmount Theater of the Deaf, and the Cleveland Orchestra, for sponsorship of its radio broadcasts.

More significantly, the 1980s heralded severe cuts in federal funding of public broadcasting. Growing dissatisfaction with inefficiencies of public institutions caused many people to doubt the public sector. Politicians began to push for ways of reducing taxes to satisfy their constituents. Amid this sentiment, President Reagan's budget proposal for 1981 sought to cut the Corporation for Public Broadcasting fund by $88 million. After numerous amendments, the budget bill finally passed Congress, resulting in a $35 million cut to CPB funding in fiscal year 1983. In response to these drastic funding reductions, a new internal PBS program development fund was created in 1985. Working together, local PBS stations contributed about $2.25 million for the development of original network programming, but this was just a proverbial drop in the bucket compared to the previous government support. *The Mind, Ethics in America, Shining Time Station,* and *OWL TV* were a few new programs that were created through this fund. Fearing that PBS stations could only survive by airing commercials, the FCC approved experimentation with a form of commercial advertising on public television in 1984. Designated as "enhanced underwriting," the FCC allowed the presentation of "logos or slogans that identify—but do not promote or compare—trade names, and product and service listings" on PBS programs. The practice continues to this day. Said Mark Rosenberger, "Betty didn't care for the logos. She tried to keep an 'editorial firewall'

While Betty Cope faced mainstream media criticism for not marketing more of WVIZ's productions nationwide, she remained loyal to her community and kept the station fiscally sound for nearly three decades. *Author's collection.*

around the station. She simply did not want outside sources—like sponsors—to influence the content of the broadcasts."

In the thick of this budget-shrinking atmosphere, WVIZ experienced another loss in the departure of *Kovels on Collecting* in 1988. Limited funds closed down production of the couple's popular show after just one season. In 1989, *Collector's Journal with Ralph and Terry Kovel* debuted on the Discovery Channel. By the mid-1980s, cable networks had begun to offer many program genres that were previously only available on PBS. The Arts and Entertainment Network (later known as A&E) aired fine arts programs, original dramas, and *Biography*, which proved to be a major hit. A few years later, A&E launched the History Channel, which produced documentaries on a wide range of topics, including military battles, engineering achievements, and natural disasters. Nickelodeon offered a whole new slate of children's programming, including *Pinwheel*, an educational human and puppet interaction show. Jim Henson's Muppets, once only available to '80s kids watching *Sesame Street*, began to turn up on HBO in *Fraggle Rock*.

Even with cable competition and lagging corporate and government funds, the PD's Freligh concluded, the money for WVIZ's productions was out there; station management just wasn't aggressive enough at finding it. The vice-president of Metropolitan Pittsburgh Public Broadcasting (WQED), Tom Fanella, commented, "They [WVIZ] are conservative in most respects; they do not do as much fund-raising as the rest of us." WVIZ's philosophy, it seemed, was to raise just enough money to air the programming. With only three week-long pledge drives and one Auction per year, WVIZ simply didn't want to wear out its welcome in the homes of viewers.

Operating as an intelligent business manager, Betty knew the risks of overstepping her budget and pursuing national programming. She and her staff simply chose to work within their means. As Lloyd Kaiser, then president of WQED, commented, "It's a treacherous kind of business. It's very, very hard, and usually a mistake for a station to move into national production. You can harm your service to the local community." For just that reason, Betty remained fiscally conservative and unwavering in her loyalty to her northeast Ohio viewers. She respected her viewers and would not put an unnecessary financial burden on them. Betty would never abandon her goal of educating her beloved audience just for a share in the national spotlight.

Sherrill Paul Witt, owner of Trolley Tours of Cleveland and longtime auctioneer of the Kwickie Board, could relate to Betty's business approach. Witt remembers fellow business owners asking why she did not expand her

"Lolly the Trolley" enterprise to Columbus or Cincinnati. "You keep it local and you keep it comfortable. You tailor your business more to your market than your aspirations," said Witt. "If you try to go too big, you risk over-extending yourself and you could lose what you have." Witt admired Betty's approach to managing local public television. "Time, talent, and treasure are the hallmark of any nonprofit. Betty had the wisdom to devote the right amount of these to WVIZ to make it successful."

WVIZ's Educational Achievements

Betty, always the educator, focused on the creation of instructional programs that were to be sold to local schools and later the Ohio Department of Education. WVIZ's school services were unmatched by any other PBS station in the country.

By 1987, WVIZ had produced over two thousand educational programs, including sixty series, for national distribution. WVIZ crews had traveled to Turkey, Greece, Iceland, and Egypt to film "field-trip" programs. Alan Stephenson, former director of educational services, commented, "Our focus was doing things by TV that the classroom teacher couldn't do." WVIZ's educational services generated a small but steady income. But as production costs rose and school enrollments declined toward the end of the decade, WVIZ pooled with PBS stations in other Ohio cities to create instructional shows.

In the late 1980s, WVIZ served 450,000 students in sixteen counties of Northeast Ohio. It offered college-credit courses each morning as well as day-long classes for K-12 students. Instructional television fixed-service channels were broadcast to schools through the Ohio Educational Broadcasting Network. Furthermore, WVIZ's educational services extended far beyond the classroom. It also provided workshops, print materials, and consulting services for teachers. An adult-learner channel as well as film and video libraries were available. A college-in-escrow program and a computer laboratory were offered to local high school students. All in all, Cleveland's public television station rendered the children and young adults of its community a remarkable range of programs and services.

In a 1987 documentary on the history of Cleveland television, Betty had fond memories of working at WEWS, but she said noncommercial TV had greater promise. "What its dreams were, what its missions were, the idea of sharing a classroom teacher with thousands of kids, instead of twenty-five at a crack, of keeping up with the population explosion and the knowledge explosion—television had to be used for that," Betty reflected. "It was the greatest communications tool ever invented."

DISCIPLINE IN THE FAMILY RESULTS IN SUCCESS

Within PBS, WVIZ was highly regarded as a fiscally sound, well-managed station, always operating in the black. Betty's business acumen earned her accolades from public television station managers across the country. Nonetheless, some former employees found her philosophy of maintaining a tight budget and her tenacity against national marketing intimidating, according to several unnamed sources mentioned in Freligh's article. But director/videographer Gary Manke said in 1987, "I've never felt intimidated. I've never known anyone who has." The environment at the station, Manke felt, was much like that of a family. "You're not going to find a place that people respect each other more and get along better."

In recent interviews, Manke and his co-workers expressed more of the same. "Betty was not technical, but she kept herself aware of equipment changes and issues. Anytime that engineering ever felt that equipment upgrades were needed, she would listen carefully to the explanations presented by the chief engineer and make her decisions based on that. She would always support us, without fail," remembered station engineer Gary Bluhm. Whether it be switchers, which allowed directors to call for different cameras, or fade-in fade-out of graphics, remote video trucks, or over-the-shoulder video cameras—all of which cost tens to hundreds of thousands of dollars—field services engineer Dick Barnick stated that "Betty always wanted WVIZ to have state-of-the-art equipment and was willing to budget for the best provided we could justify it." Added Gary Manke, "When it came to engineering upgrades, Betty was very receptive and remarkably agreeable. Whatever you needed, she was there for you."

Betty's discipline, focus, and budget-consciousness might have been construed by some as daunting. But those who knew her best felt that her strong managerial traits enabled her to keep WVIZ fiscally sound as it continued to inform, entertain, and inspire its viewers throughout her tenure.

10

The 1990s

Milestones and Moving On

F ebruary 5, 1990, was a landmark day for Betty Cope and WVIZ: it was the twenty-fifth anniversary of the founding of Cleveland's public television station. The educational broadcasting institution of which she once dreamed had reached the quarter-century mark. It was an incredible evolution. From its humble beginnings at Max Hayes High School to its expanded state-of-the-art facility on Brookpark Road, WVIZ had become a major production center for instructional programming. In early 1990, the station was producing more than fifty instructional programs for both regional and national distribution. By this time, WVIZ broadcast its own productions to more than 120 Ohio school districts and 220 private, parochial, and independent schools and nearly 60 stations across the country. The educational fare was quite varied—everything from *Arts-A-Bound* to *Your Job, Your Future*. Channel 25's programs were carried by so many PBS affiliates that one station employee remembered seeing a WVIZ instructional show while on vacation in Hawaii.

By commercial standards, WVIZ's prime-time audience was small, reaching an estimated 500,000 homes in 1990. Pledge drives, typically held three times per year, had grown station membership to about 50,000. The first pledge drive held in 1970 netted $16,600; in 1990, over $500,000 was raised.

For its evening and weekend viewers, WVIZ produced 102 hours of local programming in 1989, which caused budget costs to soar to $5.8 million that year. *Kovels on Collecting*, *Medi-Scene*, *Cooksmart*, and *Dimension* were high-quality, critically acclaimed shows, but their production costs were enormous. Still,

Betty and her team strove for superlative quality. When *Plain Dealer* television critic Tom Feran asked Betty how she responded to some viewers' opinions that the station was elitist, Betty quipped, "If being an elitist means reaching for the best, then we plead guilty."

EXCEPTIONAL WVIZ PRODUCTIONS OF THE 1990s

WVIZ's trend for outstanding local productions continued with its 1991 presentation of *The Home Field*. Hosted by Cleveland broadcaster Joe Tait, sports figures from the Indians and Browns reflected on the history of the city's sports stadiums. Tours of League Park, the first home for Cleveland baseball, and Cleveland Municipal Stadium, then home of the Indians and Browns, were filmed. Funding of the Gateway Project, which was then the name of the initiative for constructing Jacobs Field and Gund Arena, was debated in "Issue 2: Sink or Sin?" (a reference to Cuyahoga County's proposed "sin" tax on cigarettes and alcohol).

In commemorating the fiftieth anniversary of the United States' involvement in World War II, WVIZ produced *Pearl Harbor Reflections*, which

The always entertaining sports announcer Joe Tait presented *The Home Field*, a 1991 WVIZ production. *Author's collection.*

consisted of interviews with surviving veterans at American Legion Halls throughout northeast Ohio. The special also featured photos and archival footage shot before, during, and after the attack on Hawaii in 1941.

In the 1990s, Betty remained true to her mission of education, even when the topic was sensitive. *Let's Talk About Sex* was a thirty-minute WVIZ offering in May 1992 that featured Cleveland-area preteens and their parents, who were facing the difficulties of talking about sexuality. Moderated by Cleveland's YWCA Family Life Department, this special focused on helping parents and kids to find the right words and appropriate times to talk about mores and family values.

The 1992 WVIZ production of *Egypt's Dazzling Sun: Amenhotep III* featured ancient treasures from the Cleveland Museum of Art. *Author's collection.*

Egypt's Dazzling Sun: Amenhotep III was a thirty-minute 1992 WVIZ production that showcased rare works from an exhibition at the Cleveland Museum of Art. Pharaoh Amenhotep III, grandfather of King Tutankhamun, subsidized numerous artisans during his forty-year reign. Lavish treasures from Nile River temples were colorfully presented and discussed by CMA museum curators.

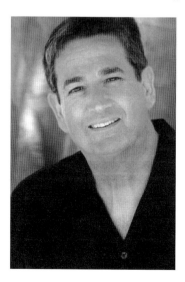

In December 1992, WVIZ presented a celebration of Cleveland's Jewish community with *Hannukah: Let There Be Lights*. This nationally syndicated production chronicled the roots, traditions, and evolution of the holiday as seen through the eyes of local rabbinical religious figures and prominent Jewish actors.

Cleveland Rabbi Ben Kamin presented *Hanukkah: Let There Be Lights* for WVIZ. *Author's collection.*

Economic Realities Set In

Although the recession of 1990 and 1991 was mild compared to other post–World War II recessions, employment recovery was sluggish. Unemployment in northeast Ohio peaked at 8 percent in June 1992.

By the end of its fiscal year in June 1992, WVIZ felt the wrath of these economic woes. For only the third time in the station's twenty-seven-year history, operating expenses exceeded revenues. Although it was reported that the shortfall of $50,000 was reached only after including depreciation of equipment and facilities, there was still cause for concern. "All responsible organizations deduct for depreciation," said Betty. "It is a negative figure because it means, down the line, we don't have $50,000 to put toward replacing equipment." While viewing levels remained high, WVIZ experienced a 21 percent decrease in new memberships over the previous year. It was estimated at that time that nine out of ten households watching Channel 25 programs did not contribute to the station. Between 1990 and 1992, the government of the state of Ohio cut its educational television funding four times, resulting in a decrease of nearly 20 percent. As Betty stated in an interview with the *Plain Dealer* in September 1992, "We operate an entire station on what it costs any one of the three network stations here to do their news programs."

For the year 1991–92, WVIZ's revenues were nearly $7 million. Over 50 percent of that figure was attributed to the annual Auction and viewer memberships. The remaining revenues were chiefly derived from educational services and corporate underwriting; a small amount originated from federal funding and rental of station facilities. With regard to the station's expenses, 38 percent was spent on programming and production; 24 percent for broadcasting and engineering; 12 percent for development and fundraising; and the remainder for depreciation, advertising, public information, and maintenance.

Clearly, one of the largest expenses that WVIZ incurred in the late 1980s and early 1990s was directly linked to the production of exceptional programs for which it had won so many accolades. As stated in the previous chapter, Betty did not want to take the risk of marketing these shows to a national audience. There was just no guarantee that the shows would sell. With no income from the sales of these programs, the station could not readily replenish the funds spent on production. Maintaining high-quality public broadcasting was, to say the least, a Catch-22 situation. The only solution was to grow station membership to as large a number as possible.

"I'VE GOT A LOT OF PLAYING TO CATCH UP ON"

Betty Cope had long been recognized as a pioneer of education in Ohio. Recognizing her strong credentials, Governor George Voinovich in 1991 appointed her to the board of Project Equity, an initiative aimed at providing all Ohio schools with equal access to information through technology, and the Ohio Educational Broadcasting Commission. Both assignments, though enjoyable and rewarding, were truly time-consuming. The beauty of her Geauga County home also beckoned, and she longed to spend more time taking care of the cabin land. Education and land conservation were causes near and dear to her heart, and at age sixty-seven, she made the decision to leave WVIZ. In September 1992, after twenty-seven years as the first and only general manager of Cleveland's public television station, Betty publicly announced her plans to step down in a letter to the Educational Television Association of Metropolitan Cleveland (ETAMC). Betty chose not to retire, as she did not want to accept a pension from her beloved public television station. Always the educator, she felt that their funds should be spent on instructional programming rather than her retirement needs. Instead, she simply declared that she would leave WVIZ as soon as the ETAMC named a successor. "It's time to smell some new roses," said Betty. "I've got a lot of playing to catch up on."

Collectibles auctioneer and Cleveland businessman Myron Xenos sensed Betty's angst over the financial picture of the station. He also understood her desire for a quieter, slower-paced lifestyle. Myron, who ran his own tax-accounting firm, recalled telling Betty rather plainly, "When you start a business, it's like a baby, and you own the baby, and it's your baby. But then there comes a time where your baby owns you. Then you know it's time to go."

On Betty's announcement of her pending departure, the *Plain Dealer* once again aired its criticism of WVIZ's management style. "The station has long suffered from its first success. Excellence as a broadcaster for elementary and secondary schools has relegated it to second-class citizenship in many eyes." The editor went on to say that "WVIZ is a national award-winner for its educational programs….It has produced fine local shows on the arts, medicine, antiques, [and] religion. But it lacks a strong identity. It can't build an audience for local shows that it doesn't have the money to produce, promote, and air consistently. Yet in an era of expanding video enterprises, public television can't stay the same if it is to prosper." Reflecting on the status of local public television programming,

In September 1992, Betty Cope announced her plans to step down from her position as general manager of WVIZ. *Author's collection.*

Betty admitted to the PD interviewer, "I don't think we've been as exciting as I'd like us to be."

In April 1993, Jerry Wareham, president and general manager of public television stations WPTD in Dayton and WPTO in Oxford, Ohio, was chosen as Betty's successor. The final Auction of Betty's tenure, held from May 1–9, netted a record-breaking $701,425. It was a fitting send-off for the pioneer of Cleveland public television. Betty's last day at WVIZ was May 30; by all accounts, she never looked back.

11

One with Nature

PRESERVING LANDS FOR FUTURE GENERATIONS

At age sixty-seven, the courageous woman who spent so many years tending to the business of television at last launched a new career in the outdoors. Betty Cope's property on the Aurora Branch of the Chagrin River had long been the pride and joy of her life. Amid growing concerns over possible encroaching development, in 1995 she sought to obtain an easement of her land through the Chagrin River Land Conservancy. As she met with conservancy founder Steve Morris and its director Rich Cochran, Betty was deeply impressed with the organization and learned that its goals strongly aligned with her own. While fields and woods were quickly being converted to housing developments in the 1990s, the amount of land available to absorb rain and melting snow was disappearing, thereby increasing the threats of floods and river pollution. The aim of the Conservancy (which has now grown into the Western Reserve Land Conservancy) is to protect the natural resources of the region, prevent deforestation, guard against subdivision, and preserve lands for the appreciation of future generations. The Conservancy group successfully promoted the adoption of community ordinances to restrict new house building to 120 feet from watersheds and wetlands. Not surprisingly, then, Betty Cope soon joined Chagrin River Land Conservancy and was named to its the Board of Trustees in 1997.

The organization found one of its most enthusiastic ambassadors in this television trailblazer.

Along the Chagrin River bank corridor were two of Betty's neighbors, Robert Solomon and Richard Roddie, each of whom owned a considerable amount of acreage. Betty knocked on their doors and convinced them of the benefits of conservation. Besides the protection of property from development, the dedication of land to the Conservancy provided tax benefits to landowners. Drawing on her astute sense of networking and nonprofit business skills, Betty successfully urged her neighbors to add their properties to the Conservancy.

Within the Chagrin River Land Conservancy, Betty not only proved to be a formidable advocate, but she was a nurturing mentor as well. Rich Cochran was twenty-six when he was named director of the organization, and Betty quickly took him under her wing. "Peter Hellman of TRW and Nordson, Dick Grimm of Technicare, and Betty were my 'Secret Mentor Team,'" recalled Cochran. "They kept a manila file folder that was tabbed 'Building Rich.' Betty knew I needed management training, and she was the perfect teacher. I had to start hiring people to grow the organization, and we had lots of meetings. Betty told me, 'Don't let them sit down and don't give them any coffee.' When I asked her why, she answered, 'If you let them sit down and drink coffee, they won't make any decisions.' And she was right! To this day, our meetings are called 'Stand up and no coffee.' Betty invented it!"

As the organization expanded, monthly check-in meetings were held between the managers and their direct reports. "Betty understood the importance of planting seeds in her employees' minds to grow ideas. She used to say, 'As you sow, so shall you reap.' We still call these meetings 'Sow and Reap' meetings in honor of Betty." Betty took her role as a board trustee very seriously. She chaired the nominating committee for the trustees

Rich Cochran, director of the Western Reserve Land Conservancy, viewed Betty Cope as his mentor in all things managerial. *Western Reserve Land Conservancy.*

of the Conservancy and hosted orientation sessions to new trustees at her cabin in Bainbridge.

"Betty had a passion for preserving land and brought her business background to promote conservation. She was really a vanguard for conservancy," Cochran remembered. "She taught me how to develop and manage relationships, grow collaborations, and how to improve communications. One time she and I appeared on a local talk show. I was horrible, speaking in a monotone the whole time. When she opened her mouth, she lit up the whole studio!"

Promoting the Park District

Betty's deep love of nature soon flowed into other community activities. Early in 1995, Judge Charles "Chip" Henry appointed Betty to the board of the Geauga Park District. She joined colorful retired biology teacher Bob McCullough, who had been a board member since 1973. In November 1995, Dr. Mark Rzeszotarski, a professor of radiology in the Department of Medicine at Case Western Reserve University (CWRU), was also named to the board. To those who worked in the Park District, Betty, Bob, and Dr. Mark were the "Dream Team." Former Geauga Park District executive director Tom Curtin reflected that "all three board members worked so well together. They came from different backgrounds, but all three were educators. With all their strengths and specific backgrounds, it was something to behold. I was very fortunate to have worked with them." Dr. Mark remembered that "Betty was very pleased when I was appointed. When I joined Betty and Bob, she felt that it fortified the education focus."

Betty's strong work ethic impressed Dr. Mark. "I very much enjoyed working with her. She was so focused on what we were going to accomplish. Betty worked very hard to protect important park lands. She approached it from a biological, geological, and historical standpoint." According to Tom Curtin, Betty demonstrated a drive for results with a vision for the future. "She was really, really, intensely interested in how we were taking care of the parks and the habitat restoration projects. She cared about how the park district would carry this strategy forward for years to come. Staff stewardship was very important to her." In 1998, Betty and Dr. Mark commenced new three-year terms on the board; they were soon promoted to the positions of park commissioners and served alongside Bob McCullough.

Top: Geauga Park District commissioners (*left to right*) Bob McCollough, Betty Cope, and Dr. Mark Rzeszotarski at the Observatory Park Dedication, 2011. *Dr. Mark Rzeszotarski.*

Bottom: Geauga Park District commissioners (*left to right*) Betty Cope, Bob McCollough, and Dr. Mark Rzeszotarski at the Maple Highlands covered bridge dedication ceremony, 2004. *Geauga Park District.*

Recognizing that education was the key to appreciating the parks, the commissioners promoted the idea of the West Woods Nature Center. True to her lifelong goal of education, Betty was deeply interested in creating a center where park visitors, especially young ones, could learn about and appreciate the park district's habitat programs. Talks concerning the concept of the nature center actually began in 1995. After reviewing the detailed plans for the thirteen-thousand-square foot West Woods building in 1998, Betty and the other commissioners realized that the park district needed to raise $2.5 million to acquire the property and construct the education center. "The West Woods was a complicated acquisition," reflected Dr. Mark. "ASM [the American Society for Materials] offered to sell us five hundred acres, but we had no money. [Cleveland attorney] Bill Ginn stepped forward and said that he would pay the seed money to purchase the property provided that we could raise funds and pass a levy." Fortunately, the Geauga County levy for the West Woods project passed in 1999. The park district kicked off its fundraising campaign the following year.

In the late 1990s, Newbury, Ohio residents Pat and John Leech realized that their new house was surrounded by the county's protected lands, so

Top: The West Woods Nature Center is the educational hub of the Geauga Park District, featuring hands-on interpretive displays and a large wildlife feeding area. *Author's collection*.

Bottom: Entrance to West Woods Park and Nature Center of the Geauga Park District. Betty Cope was instrumental in establishing this center. *Author's collection*.

Opposite: Bob McCollough (*left*), Betty, and former Geauga Park District director Tom Curtin at the Frohring Meadows Park groundbreaking ceremony, circa 1998. *Geauga Park District*.

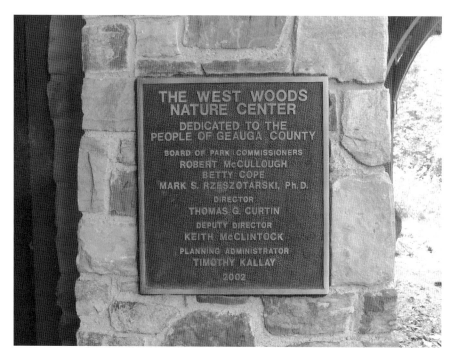

Top: A plaque at the front door of the West Woods Nature Center honors Betty Cope and the other Geauga Park District commissioners who promoted the creation of the center. *Author's collection.*

Bottom: The grass roof on the utility shed of the West Woods Nature Center was Betty's pet project. *Author's collection.*

they became involved with the Geauga Park District. Pat was appointed to the Geauga Park Foundation, the fundraising arm of the park district. As a park commissioner, Betty was already a member of the park foundation. Regarding the fundraising for the West Woods Center, John remembered, "We never embarked on a project of this magnitude before. With her background in public television, Betty was instrumental in connecting us to corporate and private donors." In a throwback to the Auction days, Betty organized lists of potential donors and assigned them to each of the foundation members so that they would call them. "With Betty's leadership and organization skills, we eventually raised $750,000, which was more than we ever imagined," said John.

During the construction of the West Woods, the commissioners met with park naturalists to plan exhibits for the new nature center. At the meetings, the naturalists proposed specific topics for the exhibits. The topics were then put before the commissioners and the board members for a vote. "Betty wanted activities and exhibits that were suitable for all levels of education," said Dr. Mark. The displays covered a variety of subjects such as the Ice Age, wetlands, a Bio-Centennial presentation and bird and butterfly habitats in northeast Ohio. "It was very involved," Dr. Mark remembered. "We worked day-to-day with the construction personnel." Moreover, in keeping with the natural resources theme of the center, the board approved and oversaw the installation of geothermal heating at West Woods. Even the heating system was educational!

Along the same vein, a pet project of Betty's at West Woods was the implementation of a grass roof. Betty and John and Pat Leech lobbied landscapers to plant grass on the roof of the nature center as a beta site. However, the cost became prohibitive. "It was a very new technology, mostly used in Europe," said Dr. Mark. "It would involve planting grasses that were not native to the area plus added expenses of waterproofing the roof to protect the building. Not to mention, maintenance staff would have to weed it. It became a matter of economics." Eventually, a smaller grass roof was grown on the garage of the West Woods grounds.

Additionally, Betty supported the "NatureScopes" program, in which the park district provided binoculars to Geauga County school students. Intended for nature trail walks, the binoculars assist students in acquiring greater knowledge of birds and wildlife while inspiring a new generation of nature lovers.

As an expert fundraiser from WVIZ, Betty also coached Tom Curtin on the best ways to approach the park foundation for the money needed for education programs. "Based on her work and life experiences, she provided a strong, guiding hand and sound advice to me. I looked forward to every board meeting," Tom reminisced. Recalling Betty's business prudence, "It always took her a while to get behind projects that we proposed. She was concerned about the expense of projects during a recession." One case in point was the construction of Observatory Park. In the late 1990s, a Geauga County resident donated a twenty-five-inch-diameter telescope to the Park District. Representatives from CWRU, the Geauga County Astronomical Society, and the International Dark Sky Association met and discussed the possibility of building an observatory. The location of the Geauga Parks, thirty miles away from the bright lights of Cleveland, was an ideal setting for stargazing. "During the meeting, Betty sat and listened very quietly," said Tom. "At the end of the meeting she said to me, 'If there's one group of people who can make this happen, it's you. You have my support.'" Just as she had done when WVIZ engineers approached her about upgrading to new technical equipment, Betty carefully weighed options against budget and made her decisions with a look to the future.

There were times, however, when the park district encountered opposition from Geauga County residents. "The district proposed that we institute a program to cull deer to protect the plants and vegetation in the parks," said Tom Curtin. "Wanting to preserve the natural resources, Betty was supportive of the plan. A lot of threats were made against the park district. I talked to Betty about this. She said, 'There is nothing we can do about this. People have strong emotions and they don't know the best way to express them, so they make threats. We just need to stick to our agenda. People will know that deer culling will eventually benefit them.' She really helped me to put things into perspective." Similar threats were experienced when a park bike trail was proposed. Eventually, the opposition fell away, and Geauga County residents gradually accepted the park district programs.

Betty remained active with the Geauga Park District until her retirement in January 2007. In an interview with Joan Demirjian of the *Chagrin Valley Times*, Betty said that her experience with the park district was "energizing, exciting, intense, and rewarding. I thoroughly welcomed that opportunity." During her twelve years of service, Betty participated in the preservation of the West Woods in Russell and Newbury Townships, Frohring Meadows trails in Bainbridge, Bass Lake Preserve in Munson Township, Observatory Park in Montville, Camp Chickagami in Parkman, the property around Union Chapel in Newbury, and the acquisition of property for the Maple Highlands Trail.

Betty Cope, dedicated commissioner of the Geauga Park District, circa 2003. *Geauga Park District.*

Betty at West Woods Nature Center, asking visitors to support a tax levy for the Geauga Park District. *Geauga Park District.*

The park district's amazing growth during Betty's tenure was a testimony to the hard work and perseverance of the entire board. Summing up her second career in nature, Betty said, "I'm not a naturalist, but I've lived in and *loved* Geauga County all my life." The broadcasting pioneer had blazed new trails, not only on the air, but in nature as well.

12

Betty's Pride and Joy

Her Family and Her Cabin

PRIDE OF THE SIX-PACK

Throughout her illustrious life, Betty Cope received a plethora of honors and awards, including the prestigious appointment to the Board of Trustees of Cleveland State University (see "Betty's Awards and Honors"). Amid these accolades, however, the treasure that was closest to her heart was her family.

Tragically, Janet Henry, who was Betty's sister and closest confidante, succumbed to cancer in 1986 at the age of sixty-one. Born only sixteen months apart, the two sisters shared a distinctively intense, irreplaceable bond. "They would talk to each other on the phone at least twice a week for hours at a time," Heidi Henry Cregar remembered. "Sometimes I would hear them argue, but they really respected and cared so much about each other." Janet earned a reputation as a talented author of tongue-in-cheek books of poetry about motherhood and family life. As a mother of six, her take on the world of a homemaker was much like that of Erma Bombeck's: you just have to laugh at life or it will make you crazy. Amazingly, Janet even penned a book titled *Surviving the Cure* in which she found humor in the rigors of chemotherapy. While their lives followed vastly different paths, Betty had tremendous admiration for Janet, and her demise left a huge void in the family.

Not having children of her own, Betty enjoyed a unique closeness with her nieces and nephews, whom she cleverly labeled the "Six-Pack." Janet

Henry's four daughters and two sons, and later, their own children, were the richest part of Betty's life. "It was just like having an 'Auntie Mame,'" reflected Heidi Henry Cregar. "We had so many wonderful life experiences." Gifts were bestowed with the typical Cope creative flair. Each year, family members had to find their birthday gifts through a scavenger hunt at the cabin. Easter baskets were meticulously and thoughtfully prepared with fresh fruit treats, small antiques, or knickknacks that she knew each person would love; however, the baskets were hidden in the most unexpected places. "She was so instinctively creative," remarked niece Chris Henry. "She specially designed gifts and scavenger hunts so carefully." Heidi remembered, "It was like, 'Let's challenge your brain, but keep things fun.'"

So exacting was Betty's gift-giving technique that each fall she held a "catalogue party" for the family at the cabin. In the age before Amazon, Betty filled a table with mail-order catalogues for the family's perusal. Each family member was asked to indicate their desired Christmas gift on the front of the catalogue, including the item number, page number, color, size, and choice of monogramming (if desired). To find the perfect gift, Betty was not only imaginative but also ingenious.

ALWAYS THE EDUCATOR: NURTURING HER OWN FAMILY

The Henry nieces and nephews learned a great deal about life from their television pioneer aunt. Betty strongly encouraged and financially supported their education. Most importantly, she emphasized the value of hard work. Inspired by their aunt's successful pledge drives and auctions, young nieces Heidi and Robyn decided to try their hand at fundraising for public television. For a few summers during the 1970s, the girls held their own neighborhood carnivals and donated all proceeds to WVIZ.

"As an adult, I realized that I learned so much from her about fundraising," remarked niece KC Henry. "I decided to work in the nonprofit field, and today I work as a consultant for various organizations, helping them to find the best approach for raising funds, and using those funds efficiently." KC further reflected, "I may not have realized it at the time, but I'm sure she inspired me in some way to pursue this line of work."

Through her example, Betty also taught her nieces and nephews important lessons on reaching goals and placing their values at the center of those goals. Heidi recalled, "Whenever someone asked her why she got involved in public television, Betty answered, 'Because I could.' Education was her passion." Betty's love for her community further drove her to reach her goals. "She saw an opportunity for Cleveland. She loved Cleveland, and she loved educational television, and she loved bringing those together," said Heidi. Moreover, Betty's resourcefulness and independence impelled her to be her own boss. Chris Henry remarked, "Her toughness and intelligence were sometimes intimidating. But we knew that attitude strengthened her drive to reach her goals." Added Chris, "If someone called Betty a feminist, she would reply, 'I'm *not* a feminist. I'm an individualist.'"

By all accounts, Betty was a workaholic; some observers might have thought that for her, the station came first. But she always kept her family in perspective, and was certain to make time for them. Following her sister Janet's untimely death, Betty grew even closer to her nieces and nephews. Heidi Henry Cregar, who was twenty-five and planning her wedding that year, described their relationship at the time: "After Mom died, she needed me, and I needed her. She broke her ankle that year, but she still took on the role of 'mother of the bride' for me. True to her form, she helped with all the wedding details."

One day, Betty announced that if any of her nieces and nephews wanted to pursue graduate education, she would gladly pay for it. Youngest niece Robyn Henry always discussed her career goals with her aunt and decided she would take her up on her generous offer. As Robyn graduated with a master's degree in psychological rehabilitation counseling from Boston University, she wrote "Thanks Aunt Bet!" in large white letters on top of her mortar board.

Betty's generosity extended even beyond graduation. When Robyn took a teaching position at the University of Alaska, Betty flew to Anchorage to help her move. As soon as Robyn obtained the keys to her first Alaskan home, Betty went furniture shopping to help her niece find the perfect dining room set.

For the next generation of her family, Betty provided even more unique educational opportunities. While KC Henry's daughter Bobbi was living in South Africa for a year, Betty treated KC's son Alex and Heidi's son Sam to a trip to Cape Town. For her great-nieces and nephews, everything was an adventure in learning. She spent many hours taking the children on tours of the Cleveland Art Museum and visiting antique stores, always pointing out the histories of various treasures. Essentially, Betty took on a grandparent role for the children, and they relished every minute they shared with her.

Betty's Best Friend:
The Unofficial Family Member

By the late 1960s, Betty had withstood two marriages and divorces and certainly wasn't looking to marry again. Around this time, however, she embarked on a relationship with a Cleveland businessman that would last for the next twenty-five years. Ray Wolcott, who was the vice-president of the US Concrete Pipe Company and a widower, became Betty's close companion and an unofficial family member for the rest of his life. The origin of their relationship is lost to history, but the Henry nieces recall Ray's presence at family events beginning about 1970. "He was her best friend," remembered Heidi. "But she insisted that they had separate residences."

Ray was very intelligent and inventive—two qualities Betty highly valued in people. "They were really good for each other," reflected nephew Rick Henry. "He fixed up so many things at the cabin, and helped her out." There was no audible mention of *love* in their conversations, but sometimes, "when they looked at each other, you could see there was an understanding between them," said Heidi.

After experiencing serious injuries from a car accident in Bainbridge in the early 1990s, Ray sold his house and moved to the cabin with Betty, again keeping separate bedrooms. She looked after Ray, helping him perform exercises that they learned from physical therapists. Betty cared for him at the cabin until his death in July 1995.

Joy of the Cabin

Ever since her youth, Betty cherished the natural world. Her love for nature grew from the many summers she spent with her family at the Bainbridge property Iri purchased in the late 1930s. The hours of horseback riding and hiking through the woods with Janet instilled in Betty a strong fervor for the outdoors. Clearly, Betty's deep appreciation of the quiet Chagrin River and its lush surroundings inspired her later efforts toward conservation of natural resources.

The heritage of the Cope family has been intertwined with the Bainbridge property for five generations. Following World Wat II, Iri built a large addition to the first small cabin, which provided more spacious and

Betty Cope, enjoying time off at her Bainbridge Township cabin, circa 1980s. *Henry family collection.*

comfortable accommodations. The serenity of the Chagrin River and the tranquility of the trees offered a much-needed respite for Iri, Marcella, and their daughters. As the family grew, this peacefulness was often overtaken with the happy cacophony of the Henry children. While the succeeding generations appreciated the beauty of the Geauga County setting, the kids found the cabin the best place for family play time. For decades, nearly every Sunday, birthday, or holiday was celebrated by the family at the cabin. Even weddings and baptisms were performed at the cabin's riverbank. The Cope and Henry families spent many a warm summer day playing volleyball on the cabin grounds and cooling off by taking a dip in the river. Some of the Henry children's earliest memories were of their grandfather Iri Cope grilling hamburgers and chicken outside the cabin. Iri and Marcella opened their cabin grounds to a multitude of business associates and friends as well.

Cabin entertainment usually consisted of the Cope sisters (and later the Henry family members) performing original song parodies on the piano. With their creative juices ever flowing, Betty and Janet often altered popular song lyrics to produce some good-natured ribbing of family and friends.

A barefoot Betty drives a golf cart around the cabin grounds at a gathering of family and friends, circa 1980s. *Henry family collection.*

Front entrance of Cope and Henry family cabin, nestled in the woods of Bainbridge Township. *Author's collection.*

Eventually, Iri sold his cattle farm and fifty acres of the property to adjacent neighbors, which left eighty acres for the family. Upon her parents' demise, Betty inherited the cabin and land. Following her departure from WVIZ, Betty moved permanently to the country setting. Her love of family and friends manifested itself most profoundly at her cabin in the woods. There, Betty continued her father's long-held tradition of entertaining for every special occasion, sometimes even hosting forty or fifty guests at a time. Antiques expert and family friend Terry Kovel remembered, "Betty's Christmas and Easter parties were truly something to behold. At Easter she hid so many eggs before we got to the party. Some of them were planted across the stream from the cabin. You really had to work hard to find those eggs!" As in all matters, Betty strove for perfection at her parties. "She put on quite a spread for the meal, too," said Terry. "She elected Ralph to bake the biscuits for these parties. Well, Ralph liked to socialize, so those biscuits didn't always turn out quite right. But Betty forgave him."

Betty's flair for creative entertainment extended to Thanksgiving as well. Every few years, she reenacted the first Thanksgiving dinner with her family by cooking the meal outdoors over a fire the cabin grounds. Wild game from the Chagrin Valley and locally farmed produce were the usual fare. The children churned homemade butter by hand. As her nieces and nephews recalled, the meals were primitive down to the last detail, even to the point of serving on tin plates.

At the cabin, Betty's culinary originality was enjoyed on birthdays as well. Money cakes were the favorite of the nieces. "She would sterilize coins and then mix them in with the cake batter," said Heidi. Nephew Rick loved her mashed potato cakes that were surrounded with dollar bills. Not many kids could boast about birthday cakes like that.

Always appreciative of her co-workers and volunteers, Betty treated WVIZ Auction staff and Geauga Park board members to annual summer picnics at the cabin. Ask any Auction worker or park board member about their favorite memories of Betty, and he or she will always speak fondly about the cabin parties. Heidi remembered that at the picnics, "She grilled two-inch-thick steaks, and we served scalloped potatoes, green beans, and

Backyard of Cope and Henry family cabin grounds. *Author's collection.*

Klondike bars for dessert. Sometimes she served lobster. Everybody had a blast." Competitive games were the hallmark of the picnics. Frank Strnad recalled, "We used to divide into two groups of Auction workers, and we had a tug-of-war with a huge rope across the Chagrin River. Those were crazy fun times." Trolley Tours of Cleveland founder and Kwickie Board auctioneer Sherill Paul Witt recalled, "The post-Auction parties were legendary. I remember one year, I fell off a trolley and hurt my ankle. I was hopping around on one foot, but I drove myself to the cabin. There was no way I was going to miss Betty's picnic!"

Betty wanted only the best for her party guests. Like everything else in life, her celebrations required careful planning and follow-through. "All her life she worked hard and expected much of everybody," remarked Heidi. "Even at the cabin, she was a perfectionist. If you messed up something for a party, she would give you a stare from across the room that made you feel two inches tall. You have to remember that she was a gourmet cook. But we always had a mutual respect for each other."

Education, hard work, respect, generosity, and hospitality were the values by which Betty lived. They were also the values that Betty imparted to her family and friends, and they loved her for doing so.

13

Her Legacy Lives On

Coming Home to the Cabin

In late 2012, Betty Cope noticed that she was experiencing problems expressing her thoughts. It was becoming more and more difficult for her to find the words to say just what she was really thinking. While she tried to remain mentally active by engaging in social events, working outdoors daily on her cabin land, keeping up on current events, and playing her favorite game of solitaire on the computer, nothing seemed to clear the fog in her mind. After a serious fall on the cabin grounds and a subsequent stay in a rehab facility, her health rapidly declined.

Her family felt that she required professional care, so they made the difficult decision to move her to the Arden Courts Memory Care Facility in Chagrin Falls, Ohio. At Arden Courts, she earned the admiration and respect of the staff and volunteers.

Betty's nieces and nephews chose to bring her back to the cabin for her final day. On September 14, 2013, surrounded by her family and her West Highland white terrier Alfie, while overlooking the river, Betty Cope quietly passed away.

BETTY COPE: HER FRIENDS TALK

How, then, does one honor the legacy of Betty Cope? For her part, Betty was a person who downplayed her accolades and honors. Perhaps the best way to remember her amazing life is through the reflections of her friends and associates.

Frank Strnad, former director at WVIZ:

Betty was an authentic television pioneer and a vanguard of public television. She was a very strong woman and a tough businesswoman. She was truly ahead of her time. The PBS network had great faith in Betty and the shows that we produced. They always looked forward to the next innovation by Betty Cope. All those shows we produced under her—she had such a great eye for talent. She spiritually and creatively made PBS what it is today. With someone as strong and as innovative as she was, it's no wonder what a mentor and example she was for me.

View of the Aurora branch of the Chagrin River from Cope and Henry family cabin grounds. *Western Reserve Land Conservancy.*

Sherrill Paul Witt, former owner of Trolley Tours of Cleveland and Lolly the Trolley, Kwickie Board auctioneer:

Betty stayed true to her mission, and she accomplished that mission. Everyone that I knew at the station had nothing but respect and awe for her.

Terry Kovel, world-renowned antiques expert:

Betty was the smartest business person I knew. She knew just how to get the right kind of funding to run the station. Others in the media respected her. Politicians fell all over her. Betty had no biases. She treated you like a professional. But she didn't like dumb people.

WVIZ producer and later chief content officer Mark Rosenberger:

Betty was WVIZ. It is impossible to separate her from WVIZ. When she started the station, it was all on her. She had to do everything—be the chief cook and bottle washer. When she announced that she was leaving, I was shocked. But she felt that she had grown the station into a successful organization.

Betty was really blazing the path for other women in media leadership. She was exacting and had a strong work attitude. She was always cordial and she truly cared about people.

Jack Neal, former general manager of WEIU, PBS affiliate at Eastern Illinois University:

I worked for Betty for ten years at WVIZ and still benefit daily from what she taught me. She took a chance hiring a young kid with no public broadcasting experience and showed me so much about this business. I learned a lot from her and was reminded when I had more to learn! But those lessons served me well.

Dianne Miller, former WVIZ Auction chairperson:

Betty had expectations of her employees, but it was never imperious. Betty treated all of her employees like family. She always told you what she wanted, and if you didn't pull your weight, you were letting your family down. Sometimes it was like being called to the principal's office. It was school, but it was good school.

The serene Chagrin River behind the cabin grounds provided a relaxing setting for Betty and her family. *Western Reserve Land Conservancy*.

Myron Xenos, collectibles board auctioneer:

Community was the most important thing for Betty. She always said about the Auction: "This is the thing that brings people together."

Betty was at the top of her field because she was disciplined and worked hard. I had tremendous respect for her.

Even in her later years, Betty inspired others to follow her ideals. Reflecting on Betty's management style, Rich Cochran of the Western Reserve Land Conservancy stated,

She was a "Steel Magnolia"—very gentle, but with a strong moral and ethical sense. By way of me observing her and how she carried herself, I learned so much. She was a strong leader with a soft touch, so creative, brilliant, and businesslike.

John Leech, former Geauga Park District commissioner:

Betty had a wonderful manner with people. She was good with people from all walks of life. Betty was a gracious woman, very articulate, and obviously very smart, but she didn't lord it over anybody. She was a wonderful tribute to our region.

Dr. Mark Rzeszotarski, former Geauga Park District commissioner:

Betty struck me as someone with incredible fortitude. When she left WVIZ, it was a clean break for her. When she started working for the Park District, it was a refreshing new start for her.

She didn't use e-mails for any communications. There were phone calls and snail mail. Park rangers would deliver packets of messages as they would patrol the parks. I remember that she drove a black Chevy Tracker with a four-wheel drive. Later she drove Jeep Wranglers. Living in the snow belt, she had no fear of snow. She could drive through anything with those cars of hers.

When she passed away, there was a memorial service for her at the West Woods. It was at the place that she very much loved. It was a huge crowd, standing room only.

A Beacon for All

Cleveland's first television station, WEWS, was initiated by the Scripps-Howard Corporation. The logo for this corporation was, and still is today, a lighthouse. Indeed, the image of the lighthouse seems to be a fitting tribute to Betty Cope. Through her pioneering work as the first female director of WEWS and as a founder of Cleveland's public television station WVIZ, Betty Cope was a beacon for all those who followed her in television.

For the residents of Geauga County, Betty served as a beacon of hope. Regarding land conservation and park development, Betty once quipped, "We don't know what the future holds, but at least it holds the land for the future." Northeast Ohio owes a tremendous debt of gratitude to the amazing spirit of Betty Cope.

Appendix I

Betty Cope's Awards and Honors

1970 to 1985	Cleveland State University Board of Trustees
1970	Woman of the Year by the Inter-Club Council
1970	YWCA of Greater Cleveland Women of Achievement Award
1970	Campfire Girls Woman of the Year
1971	Rotary Club of Cleveland Recognition Award for Outstanding Accomplishment in Vocational Service, presented to Betty Cope on February 18, 1971
1973	Cleveland Area Board of Realtors Presented to Betty Cope in Recognition of Her Selection as Citizen of the Year in the Field of Culture and Entertainment for her Outstanding Contribution, May 14, 1973
1973	In Recognition of Meritorious Service to Educational Broadcasting and the National Association of Educational Broadcasters as a Member of the Board of Directors

1973   A Tree Planted in Honor of Ms. Betty Cope Planted by Mr. and Mrs. Albert Ratner of Cleveland Heights, OH on the Occasion of Israel's 25th Anniversary in Jerusalem, August 15, 1973

1973   Purdue University Old Masters Program—Honorary Speaker

1974 to 1977   Blue Cross of Northeast Ohio Board of Trustees

1976   Greater Cleveland Basketball Association Golden Deeds Award to Betty Cope and WVIZ in appreciation for Broadcasting High School Basketball

1978   Baldwin-Wallace College Honorary Degree of Doctor of Humane Letters, Presented on Founder's Day, October 19, 1978

1978   Garden Gallery/Frame World Award to Betty Cope in Appreciation for Educating Our Children Through WVIZ Programming

1981   Radio Television Council of Greater Cleveland, Inc. Salutes Betty Cope for Services to Broadcasting and the Community

1986   Greater Cleveland Wrestling Coaches Association Award presented to Betty Cope for Outstanding Contribution to Wrestling

1987   San Francisco State College Broadcast Preceptor Award

1987   The William E. Fagan Award for Her Excellence in Leadership and Her Contribution to the Growth and Quality of Instructional Television, Presented by Children's Television International, Inc.

1989   Toastmasters Award for Outstanding Services in Communication

1990   Society of Professional Journalists Cleveland Chapter Distinguished Service Award; signed by Cleveland Mayor Michael White

1990   The Telecommunications Center of Ohio University Hereby Presents its Honor Award to Betty Cope for 25 Years of Distinguished Service in Communication for the People of Cleveland, Especially the Children; for the Leadership in Innovating Educational Services and in the Development of Her Community, and for Exemplifying Professional Excellence in Public Broadcasting

1990   City of Cleveland Resolution of Congratulations presented by Cleveland City Council in Recognition of WVIZ's 25th Anniversary, February 17, 1990

1990   NATAS Governor's Award in Recognition for 25 Years at WVIZ and 40 Years in Cleveland Broadcasting

1991   Lakeland Community College Plaque presented in appreciation for contribution to Lakeland's Management Program February 25, 1991

1991   Cleveland Association of Broadcasters Award for Excellence in Broadcasting, February 28, 1991

1991   General Assembly of the State of Ohio—Ohio Senate Congratulates Betty Cope on Receiving the Cleveland Association of Broadcasters Award for Excellence in Broadcasting

1992   The Radio Television Council of Greater Cleveland, Inc. Presents Betty Cope with the Lifetime Achievement Award in Radio-Television Educational Programming, November 11, 1992

1992   A Tribute to Betty Cope from the Honorable Mary Rose Oakar of Ohio in the House of Representatives on Friday, September 18, 1992, as recorded in the Congressional Record

1993	Billy Reynolds Community Sports Award presented to Betty Cope in Recognition of Her Many Commitments to Public Broadcasting and in Appreciation for Her Many Civic Contributions to the Citizens of the City of Cleveland and the Surrounding Community, presented by the Cleveland Touchdown Club, February 15
1993	Hathaway Brown School Alumnae Award
1993	Ohio Educational Broadcasting Network Commission—Commissioner's Award Presented to Betty Cope on May 19, 1993, for Outstanding Contributions to Educational Broadcasting in the State of Ohio
1993	Crystal Apple of Appreciation from John F. Kennedy High School Television Production Class (Betty's Most Prized Honor)
1998	Ohio Educational Telecommunications Network Commission Expression of Gratitude January 21, 1998
2000	In Grateful Recognition for Dedicated Service to the Board of Trustees of University Hospitals Health System, Geauga Regional Hospital (1997–2000)
2003	Chagrin River Land Conservancy Expression of Deepest Gratitude for Her Service, May 14, 2003
2005	Cleveland Press Club Journalism Hall of Fame 10-27-2005
2009	WVIZ Great Idea Award

Appendix II

Transcript of What's My Line? *Program on which Betty Appeared, May 31, 1953*

Key

JCD	John Charles Daley
LD	Laraine Day
BC	Betty Cope
SA	Steve Allen
BCF	Bennett Cerf
BK	Barbara Kelly (British actress)

JCD   Will you sign in please? (Betty writes her name on the chalkboard)

JCD   Betty Cope, is that right?

BC   Yes.

JCD   First of all, will you tell me where you're from?

BC   Cleveland, Ohio. (Audience: Applause)

JCD   Well, you got some moral support in the theater. And Miss Cope, I'm quite sure you'll be able to cope with the panel, but they want to know you better. So will you please walk down in front of the panel for me?

BCF Well, Dorothy's away, so I'd like to see your hands. May I? (takes Betty's hand)

BK I'm quite sure what she would say if she were here: Cut it out! (Betty walks by panel)

JCD All right Miss Cope, if you'll come over here now please and sit down next to me. You'll find out on the basis of this brief acquaintanceship that you've had with the panel, we give them one free guess as to what your line may be. And we always begin the free guesses with Miss Dorothy Kilgallen, but we have Miss Laraine Day with us tonight to start the free guessing.

LD Well, I'll bet that she's an Indians rooter!

BC Right! (Betty nods)

JCD An Indians rooter? Well, that's possible. Mr. Allen?

SA She has a rather athletic look to me. I think she's a tennis player.

JCD Miss Kelly?

BK I think she's an embroideress.

JCD Mr. Cerf?

BCF I think she works for the Chesapeake and Ohio Railroad.

JCD I'm afraid nobody has it. We'll let our viewers at home have a further look at Miss Cope and at the same time, we'll tell them what her line is.

   TELEVISION DIRECTOR flashes across Betty's face.
   (Audience: Aaaahhh! And applause.)

JCD But the panel has to dig. Miss Cope, I think you know the rules. Every time you can get a "NO" answer from the panel, they lose $5, and we keep a record of all that up here. Ten of those "NOs" and you have won the game. Miss Cope is salaried. With that, let's begin the general questioning with Mr. Bennett Cerf.

BCF   Thank you, John. Wow. Miss Cope, do you work for a profit-making organization?

BC   Yes, sir.

BCF   Do you work indoors?

BC   Yes.

BCF   Is there a product connected with what you do?

BC   No.

JCD   That's one down and nine to go. Miss Day?

LD   Um, do people come to you where you work, to see you?

BC   At times, yes.

LD   At times. Do you wear any kind of a uniform?

BC   No.

JCD   That's two down and eight to go. Mr. Allen?

SA   You deal with both men and women?

BC   Yes.

SA   Is there any paperwork involved in what you do? Clerical work of any kind? Do you use hand towels or anything? (BC is laughing)

JCD   I think that Miss Cope will agree that to the degree that she has responsibilities and there is an accounting to be made, she does indulge in some paperwork, yes. (BC nods) Go ahead, Mr. Allen.

SA   Is mathematics ever involved?

BC   No. (shaking her head and smiling)

JCD   No, I wouldn't say. Not directly. Three down and seven to go. Miss Kelly.

BK   Good evening, Miss Cope. Am I right in saying that you don't find your occupation very amusing?

JCD   Are you right in saying…

BC   No, you are not. (N.B., Meaning, no, you are not right in saying that I don't find my occupation amusing.)

BK   She doesn't find it amusing?

JCD   No. That will be four down with six to go.

BCF   You do find it amusing.

BC   Very much so.

BCF   Is it amusing because of the people that you meet or because of the nature of the work that you do?

BC   I can't answer that with a "yes" or "no"!

JCD   Oh, Miss Cope, you are taking this seriously. Congratulations. You don't need me tonight. (Shakes her head)

JCD laughs, gets up to go and then sits down again.

BCF   Do you have any special training to do the work that you do?

BC   Yes.

BCF   Do you have to have any application before your name like doctor or something of that sort?

BC   No.

JCD   No, I don't think so. Five down and five to go. Miss Day?

LD   Whatever you do, do you do it alone?

BC   No.

JCD   Six down and four to go. Mr. Allen?

SA   When you say you do not do it alone, you mean someone helps you to do it?

BC   Yes.

JCD   There is a cooperative effort by several people that is sometimes necessary.

SA   My goodness. You work in an office?

BC   At times.

SA   When you're not in that office, are you still indoors?

BC   Yes.

SA   There's nothing athletic in your work then, is there?

BC   No.

JCD   There is nothing athletic, yes.

SA   Um, are you paid less than $100 a week?

BC: No.

JCD   That's seven down and three to go. Miss Kelly? I think Mr. Allen might be surprised right after this.

BK   Miss Cope, does your appearance have anything to do with your work?

BC   No.

JCD   That makes it eight down and two to go. Mr. Cerf?

BCF   Miss Cope, do you have anything to do whatever with the world of entertainment?

BC   Yes.

BCF   Do you appear before the public in some way?

BC   No.

JCD   Nine down and one to go. Miss Day?

LD   Ah! Well, do you in any way handle entertainers or have something to do with entertainers?

BC   Yes.

LD   Would it be something to do with their work?

BC   Yes.

LD   Um, would it be well, you know, more about entertainers than…oh go on, you take it!

JCD   All right, Miss Day passes to Mr. Allen.

SA   I'm not even sure I am one. I'll just put into other words what Miss Day was trying to say. Are you an agent?

BC   No.

JCD   That's ten down and no more to go, and hang on to your chairs, panel. Miss Cope is a television director at WEWS, the Scripps-Howard CBS television affiliate in Cleveland. And Steve Allen, three years ago, Miss Cope directed a program having to do with the Heart Fund that you appeared in. How do you feel now?

SA   I'm sorry! (applause)

JCD   Ah, Miss Cope, you won the full prize of $50 from Stopette (deodorant sponsor) and our thanks for being on our show.

BC   Thank you.

BCF   John, I must say that Miss Cope is prettier than our Frank Heller (director of *What's My Line*).

(Audience: Laughter and applause.)

JCD   Thank you very much.

(Audience: Applause.)

Bibliography

Introduction

Alper, Loretta. Transcript of *Class Dismissed: How TV Frames the Working Class.* Northampton, MA: Media Education Foundation, 2005.
Cregar, Heidi Henry. Interview at family cabin, October 18, 2020.

1. Lessons from a Self-Made Man

Ancestry. "Ohio, Roster of Soldiers, Sailors, and Marines in World War I, 1917–1918." Lehi, UT, USA: Ancestry.com Operations Inc, 2005.
Cleveland Plain Dealer. "Form New Ad Company." October 6, 1933.
———. "Izant and Dibble Head C. of C. Drive." May 6, 1937.
———. "Ohio Incorporations." July 20, 1923.
———. "Steel Suit Is Filed." August 22, 1936.
Cregar, Heidi Henry. Interview at family cabin, October 18, 2020.
———. Phone interview. November 5, 2020.
Curtiss, Cornelia. "Wedded by Minister Who Wedded Mother." *Cleveland Plain Dealer*, November 10, 1922.
Henry, Christine. Phone interview. December 9, 2020.

2. Growing Up Cope

Cregar, Heidi Henry. Phone interview. November 5, 2020.

Curtiss, Cornelia. "Miss Mary Louise Williams Weds Wayne Emerson Rapp in Canterbury Club Ceremony; Off to Washington." *Cleveland Plain Dealer*, March 20, 1939.

———. "Mrs. George P. Bugbee Holds Cooking Class Twice a Week in Hathaway Brown Kitchen; About the Campus." *Cleveland Plain Dealer*, November 4, 1942.

Davis, Louise. "Junior League Provisional Members Prepare Themselves for Welfare Work." *Cleveland Plain Dealer*, October 6, 1946.

———. "Junior League Seeks Talent for Follies." *Cleveland Plain Dealer*, October 6, 1947.

———. "Saturday Proves Record for Cleveland Bridals." *Cleveland Plain Dealer*, September 8, 1946.

Henry, KC. Phone interview. November 24, 2020.

Libby, Ellen Weber. *The Favorite Child*. Amherst, NY: Prometheus Books, 2010.

3. The Girl with the TV Antenna Sticking Out of Her Head

Akron Beacon-Journal. "Cleveland TV Station Celebrates 50th Anniversary." December 14, 1997.

Anderson, Stan. "Substitute on TV Cooking Show Learns About Eggs." *Cleveland Press*, September 16, 1953.

Barnett, David C. "Pioneering Northeast Ohio Broadcaster Betty Cope Dies at 87." Ideastream. September 16, 2013. www.ideastream.org.

Cleveland Plain Dealer. "Animal Actors Provide Fun on Uncle Jake's House on WEWS." October 31, 1948.

———. "Eyes Political Pasture." June 1, 1947.

———. "Program Notebook." May 22, 1949.

Condon, George. "On the Air." *Cleveland Plain Dealer*, April 6, 1950.

———. "On the Air." *Cleveland Plain Dealer*, November 24, 1949.

Cope, Betty. Great Idea Award Speech, October 22, 2009

Davis, Louise. "In the Pictures." *Cleveland Plain Dealer*, January 15, 1950.

Feagler, Dick. "Betty Cope Is Channel 25's Woman on Horseback." *Cleveland Press*, February 15, 1965.

Feran, Tom, "Pioneer WEWS Turns 50; Channel 5 Veterans Recall Half-Century on Air." *Cleveland Plain Dealer*, December 14, 1997.

Garrett, Amanda. "Paige Palmer, 93, Was Local TV's Fashionable First Lady of Fitness." *Cleveland Plain Dealer*, November 22, 2009.

Korn, Candy Lee. Phone interview. January 29, 2021.

Offineer, Bee. "Net Shows Off for Air Ride." *Akron Beacon-Journal*, February 13, 1949.

Pullen, Glenn C. "Woodrow Wilson Saga Is Ponderous but Provocative." *Cleveland Plain Dealer*, August 13, 1942.

Strnad, Edna. Phone interview. November 18, 2020.

Terrell, Berta. "Betty Cope Becomes Bride on Birthday of Her Father." *Cleveland Plain Dealer*, July 25, 1950.

Vincent, Beatrice. "Success Story: Betty Cope Fills TV Director's Job." *Cleveland Press*, August 6, 1953.

4. Necessity Is the Mother of Captain Penny

Breslin, Barbara "Bunny." Phone interview. January 6, 2021.

Britannica. "Television: The Late Golden Age." November 5, 2023. www.britannica.com.

Condon, George. "Two TV Stations Here to Switch network Affiliations." *Cleveland Plain Dealer*, February 27, 1955.

Cregar, Heidi Henry. Phone interview. November 5, 2020.

Cregar, Heidi Henry, and Christin Henry. Interview at family cabin. October 18, 2020.

Feran, Tom. "Pioneer WEWS Turns 50; Channel 5 Veterans Recall Half-Century on Air." *Cleveland Plain Dealer*, December 14, 1997.

Kane, Russell. "Stations Plan Live Christmas Special." *Cleveland Plain Dealer*, December 20, 1960.

O'Connell, Tom. "Radio-TV Backstage." *Cleveland Plain Dealer*, December 11, 1955.

———. "Radio-TV Backstage." *Cleveland Plain Dealer*, October 13, 1956.

———. "Radio and Television." *Cleveland Plain Dealer*, April 4, 1954.

———. "Radio and Television." *Cleveland Plain Dealer*, June 6, 1954.

YouTube. "Tomorrow's Careers: Women in Radio and Television," ABC, April 3, 1956. www.youtube.com.

5. A Cleveland Epic: The Birth of a Station

Academic Dictionaries and Encyclopedias. "WCPN, Origins." https://en-academic.com.

Andrews, Al. "First Steps Taken for Schools' TV." *Cleveland Plain Dealer*, January 31, 1961.

Beam, Alvin. "Cleveland Educational Television Receives $250,000 U.S. Grant." *Cleveland Plain Dealer*, September 23, 1964.

———. "Without 'Showcasing': New WVIZ-TV (Channel 25) Gets Off to Pleasing Start." *Cleveland Plain Dealer*, February 14, 1965.

Case Western Reserve University. Encyclopedia of Cleveland History. https://case.edu/ech/articles/w/wcpn.

Cleveland Plain Dealer. "Board Rejects Schinnerer's Proposal to Delay School TV." *Cleveland Plain Dealer*, April 21, 1953.

———. "City AFL-CIO Gives ETV Station $5000." March 14, 1964.

———. "Educational Network Proposed for Area." August 18, 1961.

———. "ETV Cost Here to Be $1 Yearly for Each Student." January 20, 1964.

———. "ETV Here Makes Its Debut." February 8, 1965.

———. "'ETV Promise' Program Set for Tomorrow." February 6, 1964.

———. "Legislation Plays Important Part Role in Cleveland's Top Role in ETV." September 2, 1962.

———. "Library Acts to Enter Educational TV Field." May 17, 1951.

———. "$100,000 Gift May Give City TV Go-Ahead Soon." July 31, 1964.

———. "Peirce, Pritchard Are ETV Officers." May 22, 1962.

———. "School and Public Leaders Studying Proposal for TV." November 14, 1952.

———. "School Board Approves Study of TV Cost." January 6, 1953.

———. "School TV Group Hires a Professional Director." May 9, 1961.

———. "Study of TV Report Put Off by School Board Until Fall." *Cleveland Plain Dealer*, June 9, 1953.

———. "$20,000 Given to Educational TV by WJW." *Cleveland Plain Dealer*, August 21, 1964.

———. "Weather Still Stymies WVIZ." *Cleveland Plain Dealer*, February 3, 1965.

———. "Week's Listings for WVIZ-TV (Channel 25)." TV Supplement, February 1, 1965.

———. "W.R.U. Students Meet Instructors." *Cleveland Plain Dealer*, January 21, 1953.

Condon, George E. "On the Air: Apathy in Cleveland Shelves Educational TV While Pittsburgh Moves Ahead." *Cleveland Plain Dealer*, September 20, 1953.

———. "On the Air: Area Educators Face June TV Deadline with Decision on Station at an Impasse." *Cleveland Plain Dealer*, March 21, 1953.

———. "On the Air: OSU's Jacob B. Taylor Sees Great Future for State Educational TV Network." *Cleveland Plain Dealer*, January 16, 1953.

———. "On the Air: Universities Here Prepare TV as Educators Argue for Channel Allocations." *Cleveland Plain Dealer*, August 4, 1951.

Cope, Betty. Speech at Great Idea Award Ceremony. October 22, 2009.

Frankel, Jim. "TV-Radio: On Educational TV, Its Challenges, Rewards." *Cleveland Press*, May 22, 1958.

Harmann, George, J. "Board Votes $500,000 for Schools' TV." *Cleveland Plain Dealer*, March 17, 1953.

Hearings Before the Communications Subcommittee of the Committee on Interstate and Foreign Commerce, United States Senate, Eighty-Seventh Congress, First Session, on S. 205, a Bill to Expedite the Utilization of Television Transmission Facilities in Our Public Schools, and Colleges and Adult Training Programs, March 1 and 2, 1961. U.S. Government Printing Office, 1961.

Henry, Christine. Phone interview. December 9, 2020.

Kane, Russell W. "Channel Swimmer: Her Bold Teaching Wins Journey." *Cleveland Plain Dealer*, June 21, 1958.

Lenhart, Harry, Jr. "ETV Leaders Differ on Audience Area." *Cleveland Plain Dealer*, January 10, 1965.

———. "Schools' TV Set for Debut." *Cleveland Plain Dealer*, February 1, 1965.

Mellou, Jan. "Forum Told ETV Is for Everybody." *Cleveland Plain Dealer*, January 12, 1964.

Mollenkopf, Fred P. "Broad Plan for Educational TV Proposed." *Cleveland Plain Dealer*, November 28, 1962.

———. "On the Air: Consultant Is Sought on Educational TV." *Cleveland Plain Dealer*, July 18, 1962.

———. "Open vs. Closed Circuit: Experts Urged to Air School TV Proposals." *Cleveland Plain Dealer*, October 25, 1962.

———. "TV Education Group Seeks $30,000 Grant." *Cleveland Plain Dealer*, June 27, 1962.

National Endowment for the Humanities. "WBOE (Radio Station: Cleveland, Ohio)." Unlocking the Airwaves. www.unlockingtheairwaves.org.

Radio Guide. "Listening to Learn…A Ceaseless Search…an Unquenched Thirst for Knowledge." November 26, 1938, 14. www.worldradiohistory.com.

Schuster, Marjorie. "Betty Cope Named ETV Manager, Will Ask FCC for Another Channel." *Cleveland Press*, October 5, 1964.

White, John F. "Western Reserve and WEWS Blaze Path of Educational Television; TV Teaching Experiment Is Called Success as Reserve Official Predicts Further Use." *Cleveland Plain Dealer*, September 21, 1952.

Witherspoon, John, and Roselle Kovitz. *A History of Public Broadcasting*. Washington, D.C.: Current–The Public Telecommunications Newspaper, 2000.

6. The Good Old Max Hayes Days

Barnick, Dick. Interview. May 20, 2022.

Cleveland Plain Dealer. "NBC Donates $100,000 to Educational TV Station." October 8, 1965.

———. "The New Season of WVIZ." October 3, 1966.

———. "WVIZ Adds Three Subscribers." February 13, 1965.

———. "WVIZ Gets $50,000 for More TV Courses." January 31, 1967.

———. "WVIZ Preview Set on Disadvantaged." December 25, 1969.

———. "WVIZ—Rate It Excellent." May 26, 1967.

———. "WVIZ-TV to Construct Own Tower." July 21, 1966.

Lenhart, Harry, Jr. "Educational TV Begins This Week." *Cleveland Plain Dealer*, February 1, 1965.

———. "Schools' TV Set for Debut." *Cleveland Plain Dealer*, February 1, 1965.

Manke, Gary. Interview. May 20, 2022.

Skinner, Ann. "WVIZ Staffers to Produce Original Classroom Series." *Cleveland Plain Dealer*, June 24, 1965.

Tressler, Larry. "Memories of WVIZ, Part I." E-mail correspondence, September 1, 2021.

7. From Earth-Moving to Mind-Moving

Brightman, Esther. "Inter-Club Award: TV's Betty Cope Woman of the Year." *Cleveland Plain Dealer*, March 25, 1971.

Burkhardt, Karl R. "WVIZ Auction Is Launched; Callers Top 1,000 Per Hour." *Cleveland Plain Dealer*, May 18, 1968.

Cleveland Plain Dealer. "Bringing of Truckload of Equipment." Photo. February 12, 1967.

———. "Channel 25 to Televise 6 OSU Football Games." August 26, 1976.

———. "Miss Cope, Hollingston, Named CSU Trustees." November 17, 1970.

———. "NBC Gives $110,000 Grant to WVIZ." February 2, 1970.

———. "S.H. Smith Leads Drive for WVIZ." February 22, 1969.

———. "16 New ETV Lines Here OK'D By FCC." March 26, 1969.

———. "Study Africa? Her Pupils Visit There." June 16, 1969.

———. "Telecast Slated June 30 for Human Relations Play." June 17, 1970.

———. "Two-Year-Old WVIZ Is Growing Fast." March 19, 1967.

———. "WVIZ Moves to New, Spacious Studios." *Cleveland Plain Dealer*, September 6, 1967.

———. "WVIZ Plans Three-Day Auction." January 7, 1968.

———. "WVIZ-TV Purchases New Headquarters." January 27, 1967.

Cleveland Press. "Betty Cope Deplores TV Fund Veto." July 1, 1972.

Gould, Jack. "Public Television Is in Money Bind." *Cleveland Plain Dealer* (wired from *New York Times*), September 14, 1969.

Hart, Raymond P. "Channel 25 Special to Bring Vital VD Knowledge." October 8, 1972.

———. "Channel 25 Will Beam Pilot Show on Aging." *Cleveland Plain Dealer*, October 20, 1974.

———. "Fat, Fat, the Water Rat: Documentary on Obesity." *Cleveland Plain Dealer*, February 26, 1972.

———. "Friday's Program Notes." *Cleveland Plain Dealer*, June 16, 1972.

———. "The Little Sweep May Clean Up." *Cleveland Plain Dealer*, November 24, 1977.

———. "Public TV Financing Criticized." *Cleveland Plain Dealer*, August 6, 1972.

———. "Saturday's Repeats Are Aid to Viewers." *Cleveland Plain Dealer*, September 28, 1970.

———. "TV Offers 400-Year American Art Show." *Cleveland Plain Dealer*, December 11, 1976.

———. "TV-25 Expanding Its Signal." *Cleveland Plain Dealer*, July 15, 1978.

———. "WVIZ Improvement Steady: Upcoming Season Should Be Best." *Cleveland Plain Dealer*, August 16, 1970.

———. "WVIZ Rejects OSU Games." *Cleveland Plain Dealer*, August 14, 1976.

Hickey, William. "Channel 25 Will Begin Broadcasting on Saturdays." *Cleveland Plain Dealer*, September 21, 1970.

———. "Forsyte Saga, Popular BBC Series, Makes Bow." *Cleveland Plain Dealer*, October 19, 1969.

———. "The Unseen: That Other TV Channel." *Cleveland Plain Dealer* Sunday Magazine, November 9, 1975.

———. "Watergate Show Drains Public TV's Pocketbook." *Cleveland Plain Dealer*, July 14, 1973.

Ideastream Public Media. "WVIZ: 1960s Montage." Youtube. www.youtube.com.

———. "WVIZ: 1970s Montage." Youtube. www.youtube.com.

Kovel, Terry. Interview. October 16, 2020.

McLaughlin, Mary. "WVIZ Is Lauded as One of Top 10." *Cleveland Plain Dealer*, October 21, 1970.

Miller, William F. "Business Asked to Seed Growth Push With $6 Million." *Cleveland Plain Dealer*, January 26, 1972.

Strassmeyer, Mary. "A Birthday Party for WVIZ: Channel 25 Is 5." *Cleveland Plain Dealer*, February 11, 1970.

Strnad, Frank. Phone interview. February 15, 2021.

Tressler, Larry. "Memories of WVIZ, Part II." E-mail correspondence, September 26, 2021.

Velente, Gary. Phone interview. October 16, 2021.

Witherspoon, John, and Roselle Kovitz. *A History of Public Broadcasting*. Washington, D.C.: Current–The Public Telecommunications Newspaper, 2000.

8. Hey Kids, Let's Put On a Show!

Barnick, Dick. Interview. May 20, 2022.

Bluhm, Gary. Interview. May 20, 2022.

Burkhardt, Karl P. "Celebrities Host Live TV Auction." *Cleveland Plain Dealer*, May 14, 1969.

Cleveland Plain Dealer. "English Cab, Vacation on TV Auction Block." May 31, 1970.

———. "Hi, My Name Is Go Chubby." May 11, 1968.

———. "One of Auction's Top Items." April 6, 1971.

———. "TV Auction Set to Aid WVIZ." January 19, 1969.

———. "WVIZ Plans 3-Day Auction." January 7, 1968.

Cope, Betty. "A WVIZ Thank You to Greater Cleveland." *Cleveland Plain Dealer*, May 29, 1968.

———. Untitled Letter to Northeast Ohio. *Cleveland Plain Dealer*, May 24, 1969.

Cregar, Heidi Henry. Phone interview. October 26, 2022.

Hart, Raymond P. "Arthur Treacher's Views on Everything." *Cleveland Plain Dealer*, May 16, 1971.

———. "Channel 5 to Help WVIZ Auction." *Cleveland Plain Dealer*, April 26, 1975.

———. "Channel 25 Auction Antics Mix Laughs, Fund-Raising." *Cleveland Plain Dealer*, May 14, 1978.

———. "Channel 25 Auction—A Sure Sign of Spring." *Cleveland Plain Dealer*, April 13, 1975.

———. "Is Channel 25's Auction Necessary?" *Cleveland Plain Dealer*, May 15, 1976.

———. "Racehorse Is Front-Runner for Auction Stakes Interest." *Cleveland Plain Dealer*, May 14, 1977.

———. "TV Auction Gets Boost of $21,000." *Cleveland Plain Dealer*, March 4, 1973.

———. "Two Firsts Assured for TV Auction." *Cleveland Plain Dealer*, March 5, 1971.

———. "WKYC Radio's Lux Accents the Positive." *Cleveland Plain Dealer*, June 13, 1971.

Henry, Chris. Phone interview. October 26, 2022.

Kest, Laurel. Interview. July 25, 2022.

Lux, Ted. Interview. May 2, 2022.

Manke, Terry. Interview. May 20, 2022.

McLaughlin, Mary. "Culture on the Block." *Cleveland Plain Dealer*, May 1, 1970.

Miller, Dianne. Interview. September 30, 2020.

Paffilas, Polly. "TV Auction Bidding for Local Help." *Akron Beacon-Journal*, May 6, 1975.

Rosenberger, Mark. Zoom interview. October 5, 2020.

Strassmeyer, Mary. "Governor on Channel 25 Auction." *Cleveland Plain Dealer*, April 25, 1991.

Szymanski, Jim. Phone interview. August 3, 2022.

Tressler, Larry. "Memories of WVIZ, Part II." E-mail correspondence, September 26, 2021.

Witherspoon, John, and Roselle Kovitz. *A History of Public Broadcasting*. Washington, D.C.: Current–The Public Telecommunications Newspaper, 2000.

Xenos, Myron. Phone interview. November 18, 2020.

Auction Proceeds Graph Sources

Cleveland Plain Dealer. "Auction Sets Record." May 12, 1992.

———. "Boos and Bravos." May 27, 1979.

———. "Channel 25 Auction Raises $578,769." May 17, 1983.

———. "Television." May 19, 1986.

———. "TV-25 Auction Nets $351, 981." May 18, 1976.

———. "TV-25 Auction Tops $500,000 Mark 1ˢᵗ Time." *Cleveland Plain Dealer*, May 20, 1980.

Cope, Betty. "A WVIZ Thank You to Greater Cleveland." *Cleveland Plain Dealer*, May 29, 1968.

———. Untitled Letter to Northeast Ohio. *Cleveland Plain Dealer*, May 24, 1969.

Feran, Tom. "Auction." *Cleveland Plain Dealer*, May 9, 1989.

———. "Auction Hits." *Cleveland Plain Dealer*, May 15, 1990.

———. "Auction Success." *Cleveland Plain Dealer*, May 7, 1991.

———. "Television." *Cleveland Plain Dealer*, May 17, 1988.

———. "WVIZ Tops Goal." *Cleveland Plain Dealer*, May 13, 1993.

Hart, Raymond P. "Auction Nets Record $256,921." *Cleveland Plain Dealer*, May 22, 1973.

———. "Auction Record." *Cleveland Plain Dealer*, May 24, 1977.

———. "Channel 25 Labels Its Auction Successful." *Cleveland Plain Dealer*, May 20, 1975.

———. "Channel 25 Schedules Fall Subscription Drive." *Cleveland Plain Dealer*, June 7, 1970.

———. "PTA Fights TV Programming, Threatens TV-3's License." *Cleveland Plain Dealer*, May 23, 1978.

———. "WVIZ Begins Shopping for Shows." *Cleveland Plain Dealer*, May 21, 1974.

———. "WVIZ Plans More Local Shows." *Cleveland Plain Dealer*, May 26, 1972.

———. "WVIZ's Auction Ends With Festive Air, Money Record." *Cleveland Plain Dealer*, May 17, 1971.

Mueller, Roxanne T. "Television." *Cleveland Plain Dealer*, May 13, 1987.

Riccardi, Maria. "News Emmys Scratched, Casualty of Feuding." *Cleveland Plain Dealer*, May 16, 1985.

———. "2 From BBC Here on Exchange Program." *Cleveland Plain Dealer*, May 16, 1984.

9. The 1980s: Still Great Quality, but Creativity Gives Way to Caution and Criticism

Barnick, Dick, Gary Bluhm, Gary Manke and Terry Manke. Interview. May 20, 2022.

Cleveland Plain Dealer. "Channel 25 to Focus on Innovations at Schools." March 27, 1989.

———. "A Joyful Noise." February 11, 1983.

———. "Kovels' Show Goes Nationwide." July 16, 1987.

Cullinan, Helen. "Critic's Choice." *Cleveland Plain Dealer*, November 18, 1985.

———. "Program Notes." *Cleveland Plain Dealer*, November 13, 1983.

Ewinger, James. "Cracked Shield: Cutbacks Could Shatter Public TV's Safeguards." *Cleveland Plain Dealer*, April 19, 1981.

———. "Home Repairs Star in Series on PBS." *Cleveland Plain Dealer*, February 11, 1981.

Feran, Tom. "Channel 8 Seeks Labor Peace, Drops Fight Over NLRB Ruling; Moonstruck." *Cleveland Plain Dealer*, July 13, 1989.

Freligh, Becky. "A Case of Blown Opportunity." *Cleveland Plain Dealer*, December 20, 1987.

———. "Hidden Asset: Shrinking Violet of PBS, WVIZ Is Coy About National Exposure." *Cleveland Plain Dealer*, December 27, 1987.

———. "WVIZ's Weak Signals." *Cleveland Plain Dealer*, December 20, 1987.

Frolick, Joe. "WVIZ To Air New Heart-Saga Tonight." *Cleveland Plain Dealer*, June 16, 1986.

Hart, Raymond P. "Playhouse Catches NBC's Eye." *Cleveland Plain Dealer*, March 22, 1980.

Hickey, William. "Night Partners Should Patrol Silliness Island." *Cleveland Plain Dealer*, October 13, 1983.

Ideastream Public Media. "WVIZ: 1980s Montage." Youtube. www.youtube.com.

Richmond, John, "Jazz Documentary Is Flawed." *Cleveland Plain Dealer*, November 14, 1985.

Snook, Debbi. "How-To Cooking Is on Channel 25." *Cleveland Plain Dealer*, April 17, 1988.

———. "TV's 40 Years: Age of Miracles." *Cleveland Plain Dealer*, December 13, 1987.

Strassmeyer, Mary. "Discover World of Antiques." *Cleveland Plain Dealer*, November 17, 1989.

Witherspoon, John, and Roselle Kovitz. *A History of Public Broadcasting.* Washington, D.C.: Current–The Public Telecommunications Newspaper, 2000.

Witt, Sherrill Paul. Interview. September 12, 2022.

10. The 1990s: Milestones and Moving On

Cleveland Plain Dealer. "Channel 25 After Betty Cope." September 13, 1992.

Feran, Tom. "Amenhotep Is Pyramid Trailer." *Cleveland Plain Dealer*, May 13, 1992.

————. "Channel 25 Expenses Exceed Revenues." *Cleveland Plain Dealer*, October 10, 1992.

————. "Cope Giving Up Helm at WVIZ." *Cleveland Plain Dealer*, September 13, 1992.

————. "Dayton Broadcaster to Head Channel 25." *Cleveland Plain Dealer*, April 6, 1993.

————. "Major Specials on Big Leagues." *Cleveland Plain Dealer*, July 8, 1991.

————. "Square Lighting, Parade Shows Open Holiday Specials." *Cleveland Plain Dealer*, November 27, 1992.

————. "Subbing of Panel Forum on Sin Tax Stirs Its Own Controversy." *Cleveland Plain Dealer*, May 4, 1990.

————. "TV Recalls Pearl Harbor." *Cleveland Plain Dealer*, December 5, 1991.

————. "Two-Hour Special to Salute Public TV." *Cleveland Plain Dealer*, February 6, 1990.

————. "WVIZ Tops Goal." *Cleveland Plain Dealer*, May 13, 1993.

Mallet, Eleanor. "Sex Ed TV Show Tries to Open Dialogue." *Cleveland Plain Dealer*, May 13, 1992.

Xenos, Myron. Phone interview. November 18, 2020.

11. One with Nature

Cleveland Plain Dealer. "Cope on Park Board." January 11, 1995.

Cochran, Rich. President of Western Reserve Land Conservancy. Zoom interview. November 9, 2022.

Curtin, Tom. Former Director of Geauga Park District, and Former Executive Director of Preservation Parks of Delaware County. Phone interview. December 12, 2022.

Demirjian, Joan. "Visionary's Service to Park Board Ends." *Chagrin Valley Times*, December 21, 2006.

Leech, John. Former Geauga Park District Commissioner. Phone interview. November 21, 2022.

Rzeszotarski, Dr. Mark. Former Geauga Park District Commissioner and Professor of Radiology at Case Western Reserve University. Phone interview. December 6, 2022.

12. Betty's Pride and Joy: Her Family and Her Cabin

Cooper-Rusek, Joan. "Family Stalks Game, Builds Fire, Drinks Ale in Costume." *West Geauga Sun*, November 22, 2007.
Cregar, Heidi Henry, Chris Henry and KC. Henry. Phone interview. December 16, 2021.
Henry, Chris. Phone interview. December 9, 2020.
Henry, KC. Phone interview. November 24, 2020.
Henry, Rick. Interview. April 16, 2023.
Kovel, Terry. Interview. October 16, 2020.
Strnad, Frank. Phone interview. February 15, 2021.

13. Her Legacy Lives On

Cochran, Rich. Zoom interview. November 9, 2022.
Cregar, Heidi Henry. Phone interview. November 5, 2020.
Kovel, Terry. Interview. October 16, 2020.
Leech, John. Phone interview. November 21, 2022.
Miller, Dianne. Interview. September 30, 2020.
Neal, Jack. Statement submitted for Betty Cope's eulogy. October 12, 2013.
Rosenberger, Mark. Zoom interview. October 5, 2020.
Rzeszotarski, Dr. Mark. Phone interview. December 6, 2022.
Strnad, Frank. Phone interview. February 15, 2021.
Witt, Sherrill Paul. Interview. September 12, 2022.
Xenos, Myron. Phone interview. November 18, 2020.

Appendix II

Transcript from *What's My Line*, May 31, 1953, was accessed from Ideastream Great Idea Award DVD, 2009.

About the Author

Christine L. Martuch is a retired metallurgical and materials engineer. She now works as a freelance writer and resides in Parma, Ohio.

Visit us at
www.historypress.com